Look for the *Up & Running* books on a variety of popular software and hardware topics. Current titles include:

Up & Running with Carbon Copy Plus

Up & Running with DOS 3.3

Up & Running with Flight Simulator

Up & Running with Harvard Graphics

Up & Running with Lotus 1-2-3 Release 2.2

Up & Running with Lotus 1-2-3 Release 3.1

Up & Running with Norton Utilities 5

Up & Running with PageMaker on the Macintosh

Up & Running with PC Tools Deluxe 6

Up & Running with PC-Write

Up & Running with PROCOMM PLUS

Up & Running with Q&A

Up & Running with Quattro Pro 2

Up & Running with Quicken 4

Up & Running with Turbo Pascal 5.5

Up & Running with Windows 3.0

Up & Running with Windows 286/386

Up & Running with WordPerfect Library/Office PC

Up & Running with Your Hard Disk

Computer users are not all alike.
Neither are SYBEX books.

We know our customers have a variety of needs. They've told us so. And because we've listened, we've developed several distinct types of books to meet the needs of each of our customers. What are you looking for in computer help?

If you're looking for the basics, try the **ABC's** series. You'll find short, unintimidating tutorials and helpful illustrations. For a more visual approach, select **Teach Yourself**, featuring screen-by-screen illustrations of how to use your latest software purchase.

Mastering and **Understanding** titles offer you a step-by-step introduction, plus an in-depth examination of intermediate-level features, to use as you progress.

Our **Up & Running** series is designed for computer-literate consumers who want a no-nonsense overview of new programs. Just 20 basic lessons, and you're on your way.

We also publish two types of reference books. Our **Instant References** provide quick access to each of a program's commands and functions. SYBEX **Encyclopedias** provide a *comprehensive reference* and explanation of all of the commands, features and functions of the subject software.

Sometimes a subject requires a special treatment that our standard series doesn't provide. So you'll find we have titles like **Advanced Techniques**, **Handbooks**, **Tips & Tricks**, and others that are specifically tailored to satisfy a unique need.

We carefully select our authors for their in-depth understanding of the software they're writing about, as well as their ability to write clearly and communicate effectively. Each manuscript is thoroughly reviewed by our technical staff to ensure its complete accuracy. Our production department makes sure it's easy to use. All of this adds up to the highest quality books available, consistently appearing on best seller charts worldwide.

You'll find SYBEX publishes a variety of books on every popular software package. Looking for computer help? Help Yourself to SYBEX.

For a complete catalog of our publications:

SYBEX Inc.
2021 Challenger Drive, Alameda, CA 94501
Tel: (415) 523-8233/(800) 227-2346 Telex: 336311
SYBEX Fax: (415) 523-2373

Up & Running
with AutoSketch™ 3

Robert Shepherd

SYBEX®

San Francisco • Paris • Düsseldorf • Soest

Acquisitions Editor: David Clark
Series Editor: Joanne Cuthbertson
Editor: Kathleen Lattinville
Technical Editor: Robert Callori
Book Designer: Elke Hermanowski
Icon Designer: Helen Bruno
Desktop Production/Technical Art: Robert Shepherd
Cover Designer: Archer Design

Library of Congress Card Number: 90-71934
ISBN: 0-89588-793-2
Manufactured in the United States of America
10 9 8 7 6 5 4 3 2 1

Up & Running

The Up & Running series of books from SYBEX has been developed for committed, eager PC users who would like to become familiar with a wide variety of programs and operations as quickly as possible. We assume that you are comfortable with your PC and that you know the basic functions of word processing, spreadsheets, and database management. With this background, Up & Running books will show you in 20 steps what particular products can do and how to use them.

Who this book is for

Up & Running books are designed to save you time and money. First, you can avoid purchase mistakes by previewing products before you buy them—exploring their features, strengths, and limitations. Second, once you decide to purchase a product, you can learn its basics quickly by following the 20 steps—even if you are a beginner.

What this book provides

The first step usually covers software installation in relation to hardware requirements. You'll learn whether the program can operate with your available hardware as well as various methods for starting the program. The second step often introduces the program's user interface. The remaining 18 steps demonstrate the program's basic functions, using examples and short descriptions.

Contents & structure

 A clock shows the amount of time you can expect to spend at your computer for each step.

Naturally, you'll need much less time if you only read through the step rather than complete it at your computer.

You can also focus on particular points by scanning the short notes in the margins and locating the sections you are most interested in.

In addition, three symbols highlight particular sections of text:

Symbols

The Action symbol highlights important steps that you will carry out.

The Tip symbol indicates a practical hint or special technique.

The Warning symbol alerts you to a potential problem and suggestions for avoiding it.

We have structured the Up & Running books so that the busy user spends little time studying documentation and is not burdened with unnecessary text. An Up & Running book cannot, of course, replace a lengthier book that contains advanced applications. However, you will get the information you need to put the program to practical use and to learn its basic functions in the shortest possible time.

We welcome your comments

SYBEX is very interested in your reactions to the Up & Running series. Your opinions and suggestions will help all of our readers, including yourself. Please send your comments to: SYBEX Editorial Department, 2021 Challenger Drive, Alameda, CA 94501.

Preface

What should I say in this preface? Well, that depends a lot on who *you* are. Let's consider this logically...

Are you standing in a bookstore thumbing through this book because you thought **AutoSketch** is a really funky name for a computer program? Fair enough.

What's Auto-Sketch?

AutoSketch is the little sibling of AutoCAD, the CAD program from Autodesk...and none of that has anything to do with cars. It's all about drawing—CAD stands for Computer Aided Design, which means using your PC to create the kinds of drawings that drafters used to spend hours creating, hunched over drafting tables with rulers, T-squares, drippy inkpots, and piles of eraser crumbs. If you've ever sketched floorplans or organizational charts or maps on the the back of an envelope, keep reading...

You've heard that you can use your computer to create drawings, but need a little help figuring out where to start? Allow me. Computer graphics are divided into two categories:

Where do I start?

Paint programs let you set the color of each dot (pixel) on your computer's screen and (possibly) create really stunning full-color pictures. But they're fundamentally dumb: all they know about is dots. Draw a rectangle over a line, and the line is gone forever. Try to enlarge a paint image, and it just gets grainier and more jagged. Make it smaller, and detail disappears forever.

AutoSketch is not a paint program.

Drawing programs are much smarter. They deal with the objects that make up a drawing—lines, circles, boxes, text, and so on—in terms of the geometry, position, and size of these objects. They don't care how many pixels your computer screen can display; drawing programs build databases of objects whose accuracy is solely a function of precision mathematics and geometry.

CAD programs are the elite of the drawing program world. Their forte is to "push the envelope of precision," and to give you the greatest flexibility and drawing power through an arsenal of drawing tools.

And yes, AutoSketch is a CAD program.

Why
Auto-
Sketch?

You know (or can safely assume) that there are several CAD programs around, so, why AutoSketch (and therefore, this book)?

One of the best reasons is that nobody knows CAD like Autodesk, the company that created AutoSketch. Back in the Dark Ages of computing, CAD was solely the province of monstrous mainframes. All that changed in 1982, when Autodesk introduced AutoCAD and quickly took over the CAD market. Nobody has ever come within shouting distance of Autodesk's lead.

Is
"entry-
level"
tough
enough?

AutoSketch is sometimes called an "entry-level" CAD program, but don't let that fool you—that just means that it's easier to use than the big muscle-bound programs, and yet it lets you do just about anything the big boys can do. If that's still not enough, you can transfer drawings you create with AutoSketch into big brother AutoCAD, or many other CAD programs, when the going gets too tough for AutoSketch.

Why
should I
get this
book?

Why this book? First, because it's designed to get you "up and running" (just as the title promises) using AutoSketch as quickly as possible, in 20 simple steps. Second, you can trust this book— I wrote the manuals for AutoSketch Version 3, under a contract with Autodesk. You can't go wrong going straight to the source.

I already
own a
copy of
Auto-
Sketch

You already own a copy of AutoSketch Version 3?

Why are you wasting time reading this preface? If you don't yet own this book, proceed directly to the front of the store and buy it. Then go back to your computer and fire it up, and get ready to get up and running with AutoSketch!

Robert Shepherd
March 1991

Acknowledgments

It's a cliche that writers and editors often get along like cats and dogs, so I feel a particular obligation to acknowledge the strong contribution that SYBEX editor Kathleen Lattinville made to this book. Kathleen improved my writing a lot, especially my tendency to put most of my commas in the wrong place. I cheerfully rewrote the first half of this book when she pointed out that the word "I" is not taboo in SYBEX books; this book is much better because Kathleen encouraged me to write as if I'm having a personal conversation with you, the reader. I was most impressed by Kathleen's substantial contribution to the content of this book. Many of her comments would begin "I don't know anything about AutoSketch, but shouldn't this be..." and would then proceed to a suggestion that showed a real insight into AutoSketch. That combination of insight and graciousness made working with Kathleen a real joy, and I hope that I have the opportunity to work with her again.

Writing a book about a computer program is a complex process. There's so much to keep track of and be aware of, that no author can do it alone. If you try, you'll either overlook something or make assumptions that trip up your readers. An author needs an objective outsider to keep him or her honest, and my conscience was Bob Callori. As technical editor, Bob looked at my manuscripts with a skeptical eye. He tried out the exercises and told me what worked and what didn't, and pointed out the instances when I assumed things that I shouldn't. This book is much stronger because of Bob's criticism.

Thanks, Kathleen and Bob, for your contribution to *Up & Running with AutoSketch 3*.

Table of Contents

Installing AutoSketch

AutoSketch is simple to install on almost any kind of IBM Personal Computer or compatible. It has an automated installation program that asks you questions about your computer's setup, and then sets up AutoSketch accordingly. But first...

Some Special Terms You Should Know

Autodesk has been a pioneer in the CAD field, and when you're a pioneer, you sometimes have to make things up as you go. That's why some of the words used in Autodesk products may be unfamiliar to you. Here are two terms you need to understand before you can install AutoSketch:

pointing device The generic term for any input device connected to your PC that lets you specify a location on the screen. A mouse is probably familiar to most people; AutoSketch can also work with digitizing tablets, and in a pinch, you can use the keyboard cursor keys.

plotter The generic term for any output device that puts your drawing on paper. Originally that meant only pen plotters; nowadays the term encompasses laser printers, dot-matrix printers, and even typesetters.

The Basic Requirements

AutoSketch runs on just about any kind of IBM or compatible personal computer. To be specific, you need:

- an IBM PC/XT or PC/AT, or 100% compatible; or an IBM Personal System/2

- equipped with at least 512K of memory

- running DOS (PC-DOS or MS-DOS) version 2.0 or later

- equipped with at least one diskette drive

- and equipped with a hard disk (earlier versions of Auto-Sketch didn't require a hard disk; Version 3 does)

You might find that AutoSketch runs uncomfortably slowly on a PC/XT. (You've probably noticed that already about a lot of modern software products—they keep making larger and larger demands on your PC.) A PC/AT would be better, and with a 386-based PC, you'll really be humming along.

Also, there are a couple of options you can add to any type of PC to help it run AutoSketch better:

Speeding
up your
PC

- You can add a math coprocessor chip to your PC; depending on the type of PC, that means using an 8087, 80287, or 80387 chip.

- If you add expanded memory to your PC, AutoSketch can handle larger drawings.

Installing AutoSketch

1. Make a backup copy of the distribution diskettes using the DOS command DISKCOPY, and store the originals in a safe place.

2. Put Disk 1 in your diskette drive and close the door. Log on to that drive (for example, by typing A: ⏎).

3. Type this at the DOS prompt:

   INSTALL⏎

The installation program asks you a series of questions about where to install the program, whether you have a math coprocessor, whether to copy the sample drawings, and so on. When the installation program asks whether to create **SKETCH3.BAT,** answer Yes. (See my comments at the end of this Step on the significance of this file.)

Configuring AutoSketch

AutoSketch isn't configured after you first install it. The first time
you run the program, it asks you for setup information. (You can
reconfigure it later in a similar way if you want to change anything; I'll describe how to do that later.) AutoSketch asks you five
questions during configuration, and some of those questions may
lead to questions that further refine your choices.

AutoSketch is designed to work, right out of the box, with 99% of
the combinations of display, pointing device, and plotter or printer
that you'll find. You can use the standard, simple installation if
your PC is equipped with one of each of the following:

- **Pointing Device:** Mouse Systems PC Mouse, Microsoft
  Mouse, Summagraphics SummaSketch tablet (or the keyboard cursor keys, if you have nothing else)

- **Display:** CGA, EGA, VGA, Hercules monochrome, or
  Hercules InColor

- **Plotter/Printer:**   Epson/IBM graphics printer, Hewlett-
  Packard LaserJet, HP PaintJet, HP plotter, Houston Instru-
  ments plotter, IBM Proprinter, Okidata printer, PostScript
  laser printer, or TI 800 Omni printer

If you don't have any of the devices listed in one or more categories, there's still hope: you may be able to use an *Autodesk Device Interface* software driver for other peripherals. See *Custom
Configurations* later in this Step.

Setting Up for a Standard Configuration

1. Start AutoSketch by typing:

    SKETCH3⏎

    (The PATH statement in your AUTOEXEC.BAT file
    should include the root directory of your hard disk, which
    is where the batch file **SKETCH3.BAT** is installed.)

2. The first question asks you about your pointing device:

```
1.   Autodesk Device Interface Pointer
2.   Mouse Systems PC Mouse
3.   Microsoft Mouse
4.   Summagraphics SummaSketch
5.   Keyboard cursor keys

Pointer selection:
```

Enter the number of your pointing device and press ⏎.

3. Select your display.

4. When you see the question

```
Activate scrollbars for panning? <Y>
```

press Y. You'll want those scroll bars, as I'll explain in the next Step.

5. Select your plotter or printer. There may be several more questions asking you about your specific plotter or printer model, and about how your plotter/printer is connected.

After you've answered the last question, AutoSketch displays its drawing screen, and you can begin to use the program.

Custom Configurations

ADI drivers

Each of the configuration questions included an item for something called an *Autodesk Device Interface* (ADI). ADI is a way of adding support in an Autodesk product for devices the designers didn't anticipate. Many peripheral manufacturers include an ADI driver with their products; check the documentation that came with the device, and if it includes an ADI driver, consult the AutoSketch installation guide for instructions about adding it to AutoSketch.

Reconfiguring AutoSketch

The configuration you just set up isn't cast in stone—you can change it at any time. You do this at the time you start Auto-Sketch by starting the program this way:

SKETCH -R⏎

The -R option causes AutoSketch to go through the configuration menus just as if you were installing it for the first time.

You can also check the current configuration by starting Auto-Sketch this way:

SKETCH -C⏎

Note that AutoSketch doesn't run after this; it exits to DOS. You can also check configuration while AutoSketch is running by pulling down the **File** menu and selecting **Information**.

What Could Go Wrong?

Not much, really, especially if you configure AutoSketch for the standard peripherals (those listed on the configuration menus). Some installation problems can be related to your DOS environment variables.

If you told the installation program to create a batch file called **SKETCH3.BAT** (I recommend that you do so), it installs this file in your hard disk's root directory. Since most people set up the PATH statement to include the root, this batch file starts Auto-Sketch when you type SKETCH3⏎. The real significance of this batch file is that it sets two environment variables, ASKETCHCFG and ASKETCH, which identify respectively where a configuration file called **SKETCH.CFG** is stored, and where the AutoSketch support files are stored. If ASKETCH isn't set, and you don't start AutoSketch in its home directory, Auto-Sketch won't be able to find key files such as text font files. When you load drawings that require special fonts, AutoSketch will display an error message (and then continue loading the drawing). Either use **SKETCH3.BAT**, or include the appropriate statements in your **AUTOEXEC.BAT** to set these variables.

If you told the installation program to include the AutoSketch directory in the PATH statement in **AUTOEXEC.BAT**, you would be able to start AutoSketch simply by typing SKETCH⏎. However, the necessary environment variables would not be set. In addition to the problem just described of finding support files, if AutoSketch can't find **SKETCH.CFG**, you'll be forced to reconfigure AutoSketch each time you start it.

So use one method or the other (**SKETCH3.BAT** or setting the environment in **AUTOEXEC.BAT**) to make sure that AutoSketch can find all the files it needs.

Some users with digitizer tablets report problems with *registration* (the relationship between the digitizer puck position and the pointer's position on the screen). Often simply repeating the installation cures the problem. If you have this problem, or other peripheral problems, try reinstalling AutoSketch. If that doesn't work, call Autodesk technical support.

Pointer buttons

If your pointing device has several buttons, and AutoSketch doesn't seem to respond when you press a button, try another one. AutoSketch uses only one button for clicking, and most pointing device drivers are supposed to let AutoSketch respond to any button as if it were *the* button. However, yours may be an exception.

Finally, there are two "escape hatches" you can try—with caution—when all else fails:

- If your mouse seems to have frozen, try holding down `Alt` while you type MOUSE. This resets the mouse driver software, and may shake something loose.

- In truly desperate circumstances—when the display is frozen, and you're sure that AutoSketch isn't just involved in something like a long disk or print operation—hold down `Alt` while you type CRASH. This forces AutoSketch to exit to DOS (if at all possible), and gives you a chance to save the drawing—if at all possible. *Beware:* if this doesn't work, you will lose the unsaved changes to your drawing. Consider this a last resort.

Using AutoSketch

AutoSketch's environment consists of two parts: the user interface and the drawing environment. This chapter introduces you to both.

Starting AutoSketch

There are two ways to start AutoSketch from the DOS prompt. If you know the name of an existing drawing file you want to work on, start AutoSketch this way:

```
sketch3 filename⏎
```

filename is the name of the file you want to work on. Include the drive and path if they are different from the current drive and path. AutoSketch drawing files always have the extension .SKD; AutoSketch assumes that extension, so you shouldn't include it when you give AutoSketch the file name of a drawing.

If you want to start a new drawing, or use the File menu to open a drawing, start AutoSketch without a file name.

The AutoSketch User Interface

The AutoSketch user interface, like most modern PC software, is built around menus and dialog boxes, and so you'll find it easy to learn. Figure 2.1 on the next page shows AutoSketch's display immediately after you start it. These are the parts of the display:

menu bar   The menu bar lists names of the seven AutoSketch menus.

scroll bars   You use the scroll bars to move your current view of the drawing up, down, left, or right.

prompt   When AutoSketch asks you for information, it
line   displays a message in the prompt line. Anything you
type in response also appears in the prompt line.

memory   The memory meter shows how much of your PC's
meter   memory is being used by the current drawing. If
the memory meter reads close to 100%, you're
about to run out of room to work on your drawing,
and you'll have to simplify your drawing or move
to a PC with more memory.

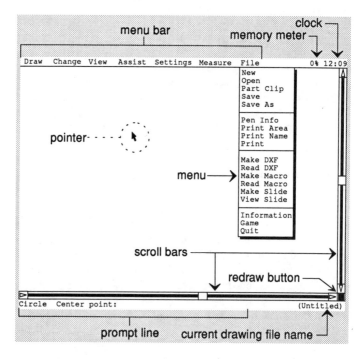

Figure 2.1: The AutoSketch display

redraw button   Clicking on the redraw button (the small square in the lower right corner) causes AutoSketch to redraw the display. AutoSketch doesn't automatically update the display after certain operations such as erasing, and you'll need to redraw the display at times to clean it up.

pointer   The pointer is linked to your pointing device (most often a mouse). You move the pointer around the screen to pull down menus and select items from them; to operate dialog boxes; and, of course, to draw objects and to select existing objects.

drawing file name   AutoSketch displays the name of the drawing file you're working on in the lower right corner of the screen. If you're working on a new drawing and you haven't saved it yet, AutoSketch displays (Untitled).

clock   The digital clock shows the time as maintained by your PC.

Using AutoSketch Menus

1. Move your pointing device; notice how the pointer on the screen tracks your pointing device movement. Move the pointer into the menu bar and notice how each menu name is highlighted (changes color) when you move the pointer over it, something like this:

| Draw | Change | View | Assist | Settings | Measure | File |

*Selecting
a
command*

2. Click the pointer over the **View** menu. If you're using a mouse, that means pressing the left button. Other pointing devices will have a button you push to initiate an action. The **View** menu drops down on the screen, as shown to the right.

```
Uiew    Assist
Last Plot Box
Last Uiew    F9

Zoom Box    F10
Zoom Full
Zoom Limits
Zoom X

Pan         F8

Redraw
```

3. Move the pointer down, over the **View** menu, until the phrase **Zoom X** is highlighted. Click the pointer.

AutoSketch displays the **Zoom Factor** dialog box, which looks like this:

```
              Zoom Factor

Magnification Factor │ 1

           OK          Cancel
```

This command is used to zoom in or out of a drawing by a specified amount. (I'll be covering this command in Step 4).

*Entering
infor-
mation
into
dialog
boxes*

4. Move the pointer over the numeral **1** in the box to the right of **Magnification Factor**. When the number is highlighted, type in another number such as 2.

Typing directly into a dialog box is the simplest way to enter information, since what you type replaces what's already in the box. You can also edit information in a box by clicking the pointer first, and then using the standard editing keys: ◄─Backspace, Del, and the ◄ and ► cursor keys. When you click first on an entry box, AutoSketch adds **OK** and **Cancel** buttons to the right of the box. When you're done editing the contents of a box, click **OK** or press ◄┘. To cancel editing without making changes, click **Cancel** or press Esc.

5. Click the **Cancel** button to put away this dialog box. In Step 4 you'll learn how to use the **Zoom Factor** command.

The Drawing Environment

When you plot or print a drawing, every object in your drawing is located somewhere on a flat sheet of paper. While you're creating the drawing, AutoSketch maintains an imaginary sheet of paper in your computer to hold your drawing, and each object's position on this imaginary surface is specified in terms of its *coordinates*.

Figure 2.2 summarizes the AutoSketch coordinate system. Each coordinate is a pair of numbers separated by a comma (12.3,-9 for example), and all coordinates are relative to the drawing *origin* at 0,0. The first number is the X, or horizontal distance from the origin; positive numbers are to the right of the origin, and negative numbers are to the left. The second number is the Y, or vertical distance from the origin; positive numbers are above the origin, and negative numbers are below. A coordinate such as 12.3,-9 describes a location 12.3 drawing units to the right of the origin and 9 units below it.

Coordinates

Drawing units don't have any intrinsic meaning—they're just numbers that AutoSketch manipulates. You get to decide what they mean: inches, centimeters, miles, furlongs, parsecs, or whatever is appropriate for your drawing. In Step 18 you'll learn how to scale drawing units to fit the paper size you're using in your plotter or printer.

Drawing units

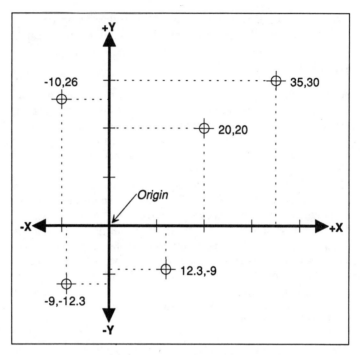

Figure 2.2: The AutoSketch coordinate system

The drawings you create with AutoSketch are stored in files on your hard disk (naturally). AutoSketch has the usual commands on its **File** menu to load, save, and rename files, just like any other program, and so we'll skim through these commands as quickly as possible. Pay special attention to the use of the **Save/Discard/Cancel** dialog box, which I'll cover at the end of this Step.

Loading a Sample Drawing

AutoSketch comes with several sample drawings to give you a taste of what the program can do. Let's load one:

1. Pull down the **File** menu, and click on the word **Open**. AutoSketch displays the **Select Drawing File** dialog box, which looks like this (this dialog box may be slightly different on your system, depending on the AutoSketch directory and the drawing files in it):

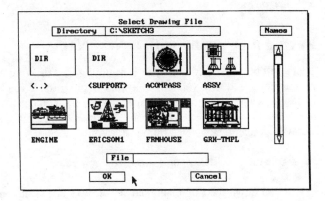

Notice that this dialog box presents a gallery of miniature images of the drawing files, called *icons*. You can turn this feature off and use a more traditional list of file names, if you wish, by clicking on the **Names** button at the upper right.

2. Click on the icon above the word **ENGINE**. AutoSketch puts the name **ENGINE** into the box to the right of the word **File**.

3. Click on the **OK** button.

AutoSketch removes the dialog box from the screen and loads the drawing.

Saving a Drawing

Naturally, you'll want to save your work when you're finished with a drawing, or when you're done working with AutoSketch for the day. It's a good idea to save your drawing much more often than that, however, in order to protect yourself from computer crashes or power failures.

Fortunately, it's easy to save a drawing: just pull down the **File** menu and click on **Save**.

Saving a Drawing with a New Name

There will be occasions when you'll want to give a drawing file a new name: if you save versions of a work in progress, if you want to base a new drawing on an old one, and so on. You can always use the DOS commands REN or COPY, but it's often easier to save a drawing under a new name from inside AutoSketch.

Let's give the ENGINE sample drawing a new name:

1. Pull down the **File** menu and select **Save As**. AutoSketch displays this dialog box:

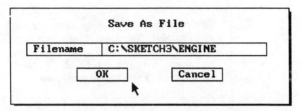

2. Move the pointer over the box in the center containing the current name of the drawing, so that the box is highlighted.

3. Enter a new name for the file, such as **ENGINE2**, and then press ⏎. AutoSketch saves the file under the new name, and changes the file name shown in the lower right corner.

The Save/Discard/Cancel Dialog Box

You might wonder what would happen if you try to load another drawing, start a new drawing, or exit AutoSketch without saving your current changes. Would you lose your most recent work? Never fear: AutoSketch won't let you lose your work unintentionally. Let's put that to the test:

1. Pull down the **Change** menu and select **Erase**.

2. Move the pointer over some part of the **ENGINE** drawing, and click. The object under the pointer disappears—it's been erased.

    If nothing was erased, and AutoSketch starts to draw a box, that just means that you didn't select anything, and Auto-Sketch thinks you want to start a selection box (which I'll explain in Step 8). For now, just click again to complete the selection box. If that doesn't select anything, try again, until you successfully erase part of **ENGINE**.

3. Pull down the **File** menu and select **New**. The **New** command clears out your current drawing and gives you an empty display to start a new one. However, before it does anything irreversible, AutoSketch displays this dialog box:

```
┌────────────────────────────────────────┐
│ The current  drawing  has  been        │
│ modified.  To save the changes,        │
│ select  Save.  To discard  the         │
│ changes, select Discard. Select        │
│ Cancel to abort the command.           │
│                                        │
│   ┌───────┐  ┌─────────┐  ┌────────┐   │
│   │ Save  │  │ Discard │  │ Cancel │   │
│   └───────┘  └─────────┘  └────────┘   │
│              ▲                         │
└────────────────────────────────────────┘
```

4. For now, just click on the **Cancel** button.

The dialog box itself contains a pretty good explanation of what your choices are, but, considering the importance of this dialog box, let's review them:

Save   AutoSketch saves the current drawing before proceeding with the command.

Discard   AutoSketch *does not save the current drawing* before proceeding; any changes made since the last time you saved it *will be gone forever.*

Cancel   AutoSketch cancels the command and returns you to your current drawing. It doesn't save the drawing—you still have to do that yourself with the **Save** command.

AutoSketch has a truly impressive "dynamic range"—your drawings can encompass the solar system, or show the details of a microchip. You need powerful tools to display these drawings, and AutoSketch is happy to oblige.

You can focus in on fine detail (*zooming*), or zoom out to see the big picture. You can also move your drawing right, left, up, or down (*panning*). There are several navigational tools to find your location in a drawing.

For this Step I'll assume that you still have the **ENGINE** drawing loaded. If it isn't loaded, or AutoSketch isn't running, start AutoSketch and load **ENGINE**.

Zooming around Your Drawing

ENGINE is an example of the large, intricate drawings you can create with AutoSketch. Doing this kind of drawing requires a way to focus in, or enlarge, small details of your drawing. AutoSketch has several zoom commands that let you do just that.

The most natural way to zoom into a drawing is to use the **Zoom Box** command on the **View** menu. This involves drawing a temporary rectangle around the region you want to zoom into, and letting AutoSketch do the rest.

1. Pull down the **View** menu and select **Zoom Box**.

2. Click the pointer above and to the left of the front wheel of the engine. Move the pointer down and to the right; as you do, AutoSketch draws a rectangle (the zoom box, shown as a dotted line in the figure on the next page) connecting the pointer to the point you originally clicked, like this:

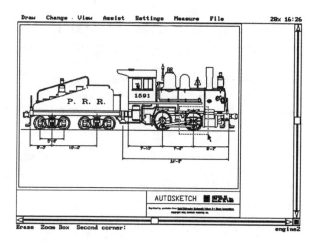

When you've defined a box around the wheel, click again. AutoSketch will now redraw the display so that the region you defined with the zoom box fills the display.

The **Zoom Box** command can only zoom *in* to a drawing; that is, it can only magnify detail. To zoom back out, use one of these commands:

Zoom Full	Adjusts the magnification of the display so that your entire drawing is visible. It zooms to your drawing's *extents*, the largest horizontal and vertical dimensions occupied by your drawing.
Zoom Limits	Is similar to **Zoom Full**, except that it zooms to your drawing's *limits*, the dimensions you declare using the **Limits** command on the **Settings** menu. A drawing's limits may or may not match its extents.

Zoom X   Changes the magnification of the display by a specified numerical amount. For example, to double the magnification (and see half your drawing close up), specify a zoom factor of 2. A zoom factor of .5 would reduce magnification by half and show you twice as much of your drawing.

Last View   Returns the display to the zoom factor in effect before your latest zoom command. This can result in zooming in or out, depending on the earlier zoom factor.

Select **Last View** from the **View** menu to see it work, and then select it again to return to the zoomed-in view.

Panning through Your Drawing

Once you've zoomed in to see detail in your drawing, you need to be able to move the view around to see other parts of your drawing at the same magnification. You could, of course, zoom back out and then zoom in to another location, and sometimes that's convenient. But most of the time it's more convenient to pan the display up, down, left, or right.

Back in Step 1 I suggested, very strongly, that you answer Yes to the configuration question

```
Activate scrollbars for panning?
```

If you followed my advice, the scroll bars should be displayed at the right and bottom of the screen. These scroll bars work just like the scroll bars used in many other applications and in environments such as Microsoft Windows or the Apple Macintosh. Each scroll bar has several parts, as shown in Figure 4.1.

Try out the scroll bars now according to the instructions shown in Figure 4.1.

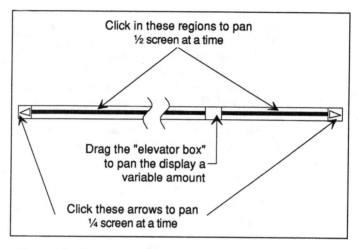

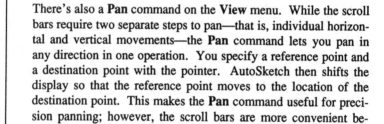

Figure 4.1: The parts of a scroll bar

There's also a **Pan** command on the **View** menu. While the scroll bars require two separate steps to pan—that is, individual horizontal and vertical movements—the **Pan** command lets you pan in any direction in one operation. You specify a reference point and a destination point with the pointer. AutoSketch then shifts the display so that the reference point moves to the location of the destination point. This makes the **Pan** command useful for precision panning; however, the scroll bars are more convenient because they're always on the screen when you need them.

Up to now you've been learning your way around inside Auto-Sketch. It's time to get down to work: in this Step you'll start to draw using AutoSketch. I'll cover the commands to draw the basic objects: lines, boxes, circles, ellipses, arcs, and curves. I consider the remaining **Draw** menu commands—text, polylines, pattern fills—important enough (and complex enough) to devote entire Steps later in this book to each one.

If you still have the **ENGINE** drawing loaded, clear the display by selecting the **New** command from the **File** menu.

The Basics of Drawing

It's easy to draw objects with AutoSketch because every drawing operation is fundamentally the same:

1. Select a drawing command from the **Draw** menu, as shown to the right.

2. Click the pointer at the location where the object starts.

3. Continue selecting points until the object is complete. (Most objects you can draw with AutoSketch are described with at least two or more points. Points (the objects) are the exception; they're actual points, or dots, that you draw with the **Point** command.)

Draw	Change
Arc	A3
Box	C7
Circle	A4
Curve	
Ellipse	C8
Line	A1
Part	
Pattern Fill	C9
Point	
Polyline	A2
Quick Text	
Text Editor	

That's it—master those three steps and you can draw anything with AutoSketch. Every **Draw** menu command uses some variation of this basic technique.

Drawing Lines

The basic drawing object is a line. For now you'll learn to draw
the basic solid line; in Step 11 you'll learn how to draw objects
with dotted, dashed, and many other line styles.

1. Pull down the **Draw** menu and select **Line**.

2. Down in the prompt line, AutoSketch asks you to `Enter
    point`, which means that you should move the pointer to
    where the line will begin, and click the pointer button. In
    this case, click the pointer near one of the corners of the
    screen, release the button, and move the pointer toward the
    opposite corner. As you do this, notice that AutoSketch
    draws a continuous line between the first point and the
    pointer. This is called a *rubberband* line, because it seems
    to stretch like a rubberband.

3. The prompt changes to `To point`; AutoSketch wants to
    know where the line will end. Pick a point anywhere you
    want, and click the pointer. AutoSketch then draws the
    real line (as opposed to the rubberband line) between the
    two points you picked.

    The process of drawing a line can be summarized like this:

That's all there is to it. For the rest of this Step we'll survey the basic
drawing commands of AutoSketch. A note on terminology: from
now on I'll refer to positioning the pointer and clicking as *picking a
point*. For the rest of this book I'll use a shorthand notation in the
numbered steps, in which Courier text shows you the prompt
AutoSketch displays in the prompt line. The instructions after that
will tell you how to respond.

Drawing Boxes

A *box* is AutoSketch terminology for any rectangle. Draw it by specifying two opposite corners.

1. Select **Box** from the **Draw** menu.

2. `First corner:` Pick the first point specifying one corner. As you move the pointer away from this point, AutoSketch draws a rubberband outline of the rectangle.

3. `Second corner:` Pick the second point specifying the opposite corner.

The process of drawing a box can be summarized like this:

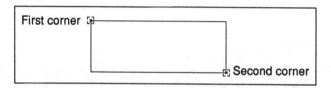

First corner

Second corner

Drawing Circles

You draw circles with AutoSketch by first specifying the center of the circle, and then a point on the circle (on its circumference).

1. Select **Circle** from the **Draw** menu.

2. `Center point:` Pick the first point specifying the center of the circle. As you move the pointer away from the center, AutoSketch draws a rubberband outline of the circle, which grows larger as you move away from the center. This rubberband outline isn't smooth (so that AutoSketch can draw it faster), but don't worry: the circle you ultimately draw will be mathematically perfect.

3. `Point on circle:` Pick a second point. AutoSketch will draw the circle through this point, with the first point as its center. As a result, the distance from the first point to the second point is the radius of the circle.

The process of drawing a circle can be summarized like this:

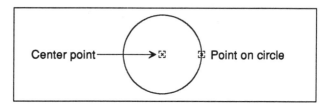

AutoSketch draws perfect circles. (They're generated mathematically from the points you specify.) However, some computer displays don't have uniform vertical and horizontal sizes, so on the screen the circle may look more like an ellipse than a circle. Don't worry—when you plot the drawing the circle will be a circle.

Ellipses

The ability to draw ellipses is new in Version 3 of AutoSketch. While users of earlier versions could get by without them, you'll be delighted with all the things you can draw with ellipses. They're fundamental to perspective drawing (since they can represent a circle seen at an angle), and in Step 9 you'll learn how to cut pieces from an ellipse and use them as curves.

The designers of AutoSketch weren't content to just add the ability to draw ellipses; they've given you three different methods you can use to draw ellipses, each useful in different situations. You'll learn the basic method (the one that AutoSketch uses by default) in this book. Refer to the AutoSketch manuals to learn about the others.

The basic method involves specifying three points: the center of the ellipse and two axis endpoints. One axis is the distance from the center along the longest dimension of the ellipse, and the other axis is the distance along the shortest dimension of the ellipse. If you keep in mind that a circle is just a special case of an ellipse, with both axes the same length, you can visualize the difference in the length of the axes as the amount by which a circle is "squashed" to create an ellipse.

1. Select **Ellipse** from the **Draw** menu.

2. `Center of ellipse:` Pick a point near the center of the screen. As you move the pointer away from the center, AutoSketch draws a rubberband line. (It can't draw the outline of the ellipse yet because it doesn't have the other axis endpoint.)

3. `Axis endpoint:` Pick a point to the right or left of the center. Now, as you move away from this point, Auto-Sketch can begin to draw the outline of the ellipse. Like the circle, this outline will look a little rough—it's just an approximation of the final shape.

4. `Other axis distance:` Pick the final point above or below the center. AutoSketch draws the ellipse after you specify this point.

Drawing ellipses using the basic method can be summarized like this:

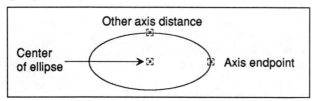

Drawing Arcs

Arcs are portions of a circle. You draw an arc by specifying three points: its starting point, a point somewhere on it, and it's ending point. AutoSketch will then compute the arc that will pass through all three points.

1. Select **Arc** from the **Draw** menu.

2. `Start point:` Pick a point specifying the beginning of the arc.

3. `Point on arc:` Pick a second point. As you move the pointer away from the second point, AutoSketch displays a rough approximation of the shape of the arc.

Before you place the third point, experiment with moving the pointer around and watch the shape of the arc that AutoSketch draws. The arc is very flat when all three points are close to being in a straight line. When you move the pointer close to the first point, the arc almost makes a full circle.

4. Endpoint: Pick the third point.

Drawing an arc can be summarized like this:

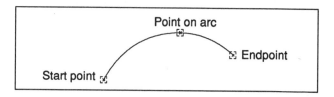

Point on arc

Endpoint

Start point

Arcs can be a bit tricky, especially if you have turned on one of the drawings aids that restricts pointer movement (explained in Step 7). That's because the middle point might not lie on a nice even location. In many situations you might find it easier to start with a circle, and then cut away the part you don't need to leave the arc you want. This cutting operation is called *breaking* an object, and you'll learn about it in Step 9.

Drawing Curves

You can draw curves of almost any complexity with AutoSketch. It uses a method of curve-drawing called *cubic B-splines*, but don't let that technical term get in the way: the concept is intuitive and direct.

Imagine you've pinned a piece of elastic cord to a board (see Figure 5.1). Then you put more pins above and below the cord, and tie short lengths of nonelastic string from the pins to the elastic cord. Each piece of string warps the elastic in a particular direction. That's the principle behind a cubic B-spline. The pins and strings warping the elastic are known as *control points*, and the farther they are from the center line between the ends of the curve, the more the associated segment of the curve bends.

While you're drawing the curve, AutoSketch doesn't display the curve itself (that takes some sophisticated math, and would be very slow). Rather, AutoSketch displays a series of straight lines, called a *frame*, connecting each control point. When you pick the final point, AutoSketch draws the curve.

1. Select **Curve** from the **Draw** menu.

2. First point: Pick the first endpoint of the curve. As you move the pointer away, AutoSketch draws a straight rubberband line back to the first point (the first part of the frame).

3. To point: Pick several more points above and below the level of the first point. As you do this, AutoSketch draws the frame segments connecting these control points.

4. Click the pointer twice rapidly at the final point. This *double-click* signals to AutoSketch that the curve is done. AutoSketch then computes and draws the curve based on the series of control points you picked. (Take note of this double-click method of terminating a drawing operation—it's used to end all objects that don't have a fixed number of points).

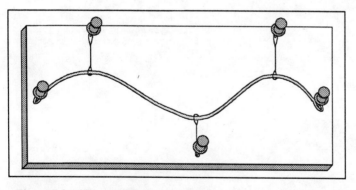

Figure 5.1: How AutoSketch draws a curve

You may notice that the curve isn't quite smooth even after it's drawn (unlike circles, ellipses, and arcs). That's because the curve is actually a series of very short straight line segments. You can control the smoothness of curves (how many straight lines make up a given section of curve) by selecting **Curve** from the **Settings** menu and entering a different value for drawing segments in the **Curve** dialog box.

A curve can have no more than 200 control points (including the beginning and ending points). AutoSketch will let you know with an error message if you ever reach that many points in a curve. If this happens, you can draw the curve you need in two parts, as two separate curves. You can then group several curves to keep them together. (I'll cover grouping objects in Step 10.)

AutoSketch Version 3 has a fairly complete set of tools for handling text. You can add single lines of text to your drawing, or several lines at a time with the new text editor. You can control the text's alignment, rotation on the page, and size and appearance. Auto-Sketch includes a number of text fonts (typefaces), and you can add more from third parties.

However, AutoSketch isn't a word processor. Don't expect Auto-Sketch to provide fancy features like word-wrap, or to use the nice fonts built into your printer, if you're using a printer for output. AutoSketch *draws* all characters, and therefore they look like CAD text. In other words, they resemble the way a draftsman would draw text by hand using a template.

Quick Text

The **Quick Text** command on the **Draw** menu lets you draw a single line of text. Try it now. (If you have another drawing loaded, select **New** from the **File** menu to clear the drawing workspace. Save the current drawing if necessary.)

Drawing single lines of text

1. Select **Quick Text** from the **Draw** menu.

2. Enter point: Pick a point on the display.

3. Enter text: Type something.

    As you type, AutoSketch draws your text on the screen, and also displays it in the prompt line. When you get to the end of the line, press ⏎. AutoSketch erases and redraws the text, and clears the prompt line for another line of text. You can repeat this process as many times as necessary, until you select another command.

Using Different Fonts

Better-looking text

In the last exercise you saw that, by default, AutoSketch used a very basic font to draw your text. It's called Standard, and it draws quickly on the screen because it's so simple. However, you'll probably want a nicer-looking font for your drawings, and AutoSketch can accommodate you. Figures 6.1 and 6.2 show the built-in font options.

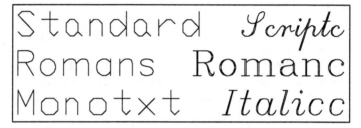

Figure 6.1: Built-in text fonts

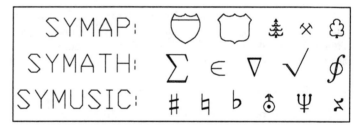

Figure 6.2: Built-in symbol fonts

1. Select **Text** from the **Settings** menu. AutoSketch displays the **Text and Font Modes** dialog box, which looks like this:

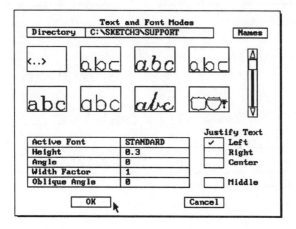

2. This is another icon-based selection box, like the **Open File** dialog box. The similarity is significant: AutoSketch stores its fonts in *shape* files (analogous to drawing files, in that they tell AutoSketch how to draw the characters in the font). The icons show samples of each available font. Click the fourth sample; the name **ROMANC** will appear in a box next to the legend **Active Font**.

3. Click **OK** to put away this dialog box.

4. Notice that the **Quick Text** command is still selected. Select another point, and draw text in this new font.

Controlling Text Alignment

So far, the text you've drawn has lined up to the right of, and above, the point you picked. That's the default setting, but you might want to draw text with different alignments. This is useful if your text must be lined up in a specific relation to an object in your drawing, such as a label to the left of an object. Figure 6.3 shows how AutoSketch can align text.

Let's assume you want to draw text centered horizontally and vertically around a point.

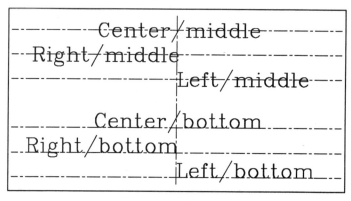

Figure 6.3: Text alignment

1. Select **Text** from the **Settings** menu.

2. In the dialog box, under the heading **Justify Text** in the lower right, click on **Center**; this controls the horizontal alignment. Click on **Middle**; this controls the vertical alignment. Click **OK** to put away the dialog box.

3. (**Quick Text** should still be selected.) Pick another point and draw a line of text. Notice that, as you type, AutoSketch draws the text aligned to the right and above the point you picked. This time however, when you press 🠰, AutoSketch redraws the text as you specified, aligned horizontally and vertically around the pick point.

Drawing Text with the Text Editor

Drawing multiple lines of text

A new feature of AutoSketch Version 3 is a multi-line text editor. You can use the text editor both to create new text and to change existing text. Single-line text is useful for labels and legends, but the text editor is indispensable for creating blocks of text such as notes or instructions. Let's try it.

1. Select **Text Editor** from the **Draw** menu.

2. Enter point: Pick the point where the block of text will begin. After you do so, AutoSketch displays the **Text Editor** window, which looks like this:

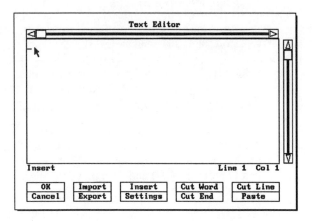

Take a moment to look over the text editor. The large window is where you work with text. The buttons at the bottom control various text editor functions.

Cut Word, Cut End, Cut Line and Paste These buttons lets you move text around within the text editor window. I'll describe cut and paste operations a bit later.

Insert (and Typeover) This button controls whether new text you type moves existing text to the right (**Insert**), or replaces existing text (**Typeover**). If you click this button, its legend changes to **Typeover**; clicking it again changes it back to **Insert**.

Settings This button displays the **Text and Font Modes** dialog box so that you can change text settings on the fly.

Import   These buttons let you read text into the editor
and   from an external text file (a file that contains only
Export   ASCII characters), and write out text from the text
editor into an external file.

3.   Type several lines of text. Press ⏎ at the end of each line. Try experimenting a bit with the text editor:

   - Click the pointer in the text and type new characters in insert mode. Then click the **Insert** button to change to typeover mode to see what happens.

Editing text with the keyboard

   - You can also use the keyboard to edit text. The cursor keys move the cursor around in the text. Holding down Ctrl while you press the ← and → keys moves you a word at a time. PgUp and PgDn move the display a window-full at a time. ←Backspace and Del work in the usual way.

   - Click the **Settings** button to display the **Text and Font Modes** dialog box. Change the text alignment back to **Left**, and turn off **Middle** by clicking on it. Try selecting a different font. Then click **OK** to return to the **Text Editor** window.

4.   When you're done, click **OK**. AutoSketch draws your text, which should be centered horizontally and vertically, unless you've changed the alignment settings.

Cutting and Pasting Text

The **Cut Word, Cut End, Cut Line** and **Paste** buttons work together to let you rearrange text within the text editor. Click one of the **Cut** buttons to remove text from the editor window (a word at a time, to the end of the current line, or an entire line), and store it in a temporary holding area. Then use the **Paste** button to insert the text somewhere else. In other words, AutoSketch has a facility very similar to the clipboard you might have used in Microsoft Windows or on the Apple Macintosh.

Figure 6.4 summarizes how the cut and paste facility works.

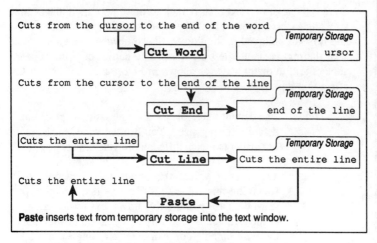

Figure 6.4: AutoSketch's cut and paste facility

Changing Text with the Text Editor

You can also use the text editor to change existing text. Try it on the block of text you just entered.

1. Select **Text Editor** from the **Change** menu (*not* the **Draw** menu; this version of the **Text Editor** command is for changing text).

2. Select object: Pick your existing text by clicking on it. AutoSketch displays the **Text Editor** window, with the selected text loaded into the main window.

3. Change the text. This is a good opportunity to try out the cut-and-paste buttons, as well as to exercise the editing keys.

4. When you're done experimenting, click **OK** to put away the text editor. AutoSketch redraws the block of text with all your changes.

Advanced Text Formatting

So far you've drawn text in its default form. It appears in the default size, angle (that is, your text has been horizontal), and normal width, and it is not obliqued (obliquing text is somewhat like using *italic* text; the text is slanted left or right). You can change the appearance of text in many ways, as shown in Figure 6.5. These options affect text this way:

Height The default value of 0.3 drawing units matches the default drawing size. You'll often want text larger or smaller to match different drawing scales.

Angle The default value, 0°, draws text horizontally. Changing this value to 90° draws text straight up from the base point, 180° draws text upside down to the left, and 270° draws text straight down from the base point. You can enter any angle from 0° to 360°.

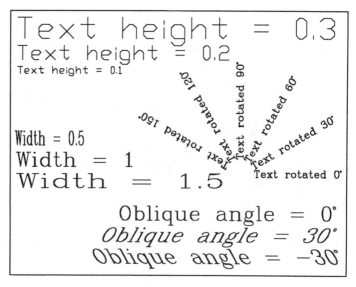

Figure 6.5: Text appearance options

Width The default value of 1 draws text at its normal width.
Factor A larger value stretches text (making it wider), while
a smaller value squeezes text (making it narrower).

Oblique The default value of 0 draws text that stands upright.
Angle A positive oblique angle tilts text to the right, while
a negative angle tilts text to the left. You can use
this setting to make text resemble *italics*.

All text settings apply to an entire text object; you can't change
the appearance of individual characters. If you need to mix text
of different appearances, create each piece of text individually,
and then line them up so they look like they're all part of the same
text object.

Let's experiment by changing several text appearance options at
once:

1. Select **Text** from the **Settings** menu.

2. In the **Text and Font Modes** dialog box, enter:

   - .75 for the new text height

   - 45 for the new text angle

   - 2 for the new text width factor

   - −30 for the new text oblique angle

   Click **OK** to put away this dialog box.

3. Select **Quick Text** from the **Draw** menu, pick a point, draw a
   line of text, and press 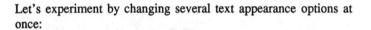.

Special Text Characters

*Under-
scoring
and
over-
scoring
text*

You can embed control codes in your text to produce special characters, underlining, and overscoring. Each control code starts with two
percent signs (%%). When you want to draw a single percent sign,
you have to type three of them (%%%). Figure 6.6 shows the
special character codes.

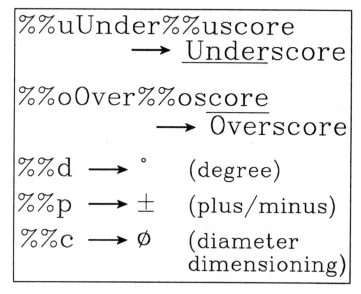

Figure 6.6: Special characters

Precision Drawing

You didn't get AutoSketch to produce sloppy drawings—CAD programs are supposed to let you easily create uncompromisingly precise drawings. So what can AutoSketch do for you? A lot! AutoSketch's precision-drawing capabilities rest on three foundations:

- *Coordinates:* AutoSketch can deal with coordinates as large as $\pm 1 \times 10^{36}$, and a coordinate can have up to six digits of precision to the right of the decimal point. You can express very large coordinates using scientific notation. For example, 53,692,000 can be entered as 5.3692e7. You can also specify a coordinate in terms of its distance and direction from the previous coordinate.

- *Visual aids:* The coordinate display reads out the location of the pointer as you move it around the display. You can turn on a grid of dots on the display to orient yourself visually. Snap mode can restrict pointer movement to specific intervals (not necessarily on the grid). Ortho mode lets you draw lines restricted to the absolute horizontal or vertical.

- *Attach modes:* A rich set of attachment aids lets you locate features of objects. For example, you can attach a line to the absolute center of a circle, or you can "anchor" one axis of an ellipse to the midpoint of one edge of a box.

I'll explain these features individually, and then tie them all together at the end of this Step with a comprehensive exercise.

Exploiting Coordinates

Step 2 described AutoSketch's coordinate system. The keys to exploiting AutoSketch's precision coordinates are displaying coordinates and entering them through the keyboard.

The Coordinate Displays

AutoSketch has two coordinate displays you can turn on; one display is on screen all the time and shows where the pointer is, and the other turns itself on when you start to draw an object. First, you must turn on the coordinate location display:

Toggled functions

1. Select **Coords** from the **Assist** menu. There's no dialog box; as soon as you release the pointer button your choice goes into effect.

   Coords, like most of the **Assist** commands, is a *toggled* function: the first time you select a toggled function it's turned on, the second time it's turned off, and a third time turns it back on, and so on forever. If you pull down the **Assist** menu again, you'll see that there's now a checkmark next to **Coords**. More to the point, the prompt line now contains the basic coordinate display. It follows the standard coordinate format of *X,Y*.

2. Move the pointer around, and watch the coordinate display. This will help you get an intuitive feel for coordinates.

The second coordinate display swings into action after you pick the first point of an object. Its purpose is to indicate the direction and bearing of the second point from the first, and subsequent points in a multiple-point object from previous points. Let's try it:

1. Select **Line** from the **Draw** menu. Pick the first point in the center of the display, and then move the pointer away.

2. Look at the upper right corner of the screen: another coordinate display has replaced the memory meter and clock. Move the pointer around the screen and watch what this second display shows.

Polar coordinates

These numbers don't look like the *X,Y* coordinates in the prompt line, do they? They're called *polar coordinates*, and this display is sometimes called the *polar coordinate display*. Polar coordinates show the pointer's position relative to the previous point using a *p(distance,bearing)* notation. (The "p" at the beginning signifies polar notation.) Distance is in drawing units, and bearing is in degrees. Bearings start with 0° to the right, and angles proceed counter-clockwise from there. (Don't confuse this system with map notation; in this system, east would be 0° and south is at 270°). More on polar coordinates later.

Entering Coordinates through the Keyboard

All of AutoSketch's precision in handling coordinates would be useless if you could only specify locations with the pointer (try it and see; you'll find that your computer's display doesn't offer enough resolution to let you find a given point with any accuracy, let alone return to the point again later). Luckily, you can enter coordinates through the keyboard to the full precision AutoSketch supports. The basic method is simple: any time the prompt line asks for a point, just type it in using the standard *X,Y* notation. Try it:

1. Select **Line** from the **Draw** menu.

    By the way, you should have been in the middle of a line drawing operation from the last exercise (you'd specified the first point, but not the second). Selecting the **Line** command again canceled the previous command without completing it. You can cancel almost any operation in midstream by selecting another command.

2. `Enter point:` Type `1.0137,2.9119`. Notice that a rubberband line appears with one end anchored at coordinates 1.0137,2.9119 near the lower left of the screen.

3. `To point:` Type `8,5`. AutoSketch draws a line from 1.0137,2.9119 to 8,5 (and you never had to move the pointer).

As you can see, it's nearly impossible to pick locations such as 1.0137,2.9119 with the pointer alone; you need the keyboard.

You can create precision drawings of almost anything entering these *absolute* coordinates through the keyboard, but you'd spend a lot of time punching keys on a calculator to compute the location of one point in *relation* to another. Again, AutoSketch comes to the rescue with two ways of specifying a location relative to the previous point. Figure 7.1 summarizes the coordinate entry methods.

Canceling a command

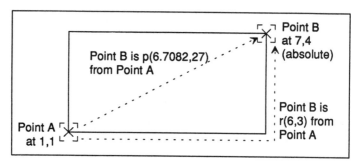

Figure 7.1: Relative coordinate systems

Relative coordinates

The first method is called, logically enough, *relative coordinates*. By putting *X,Y* coordinates in parentheses and putting the letter "R" (either upper- or lowercase) in front, you tell AutoSketch that you want your next point to be *X* units horizontally and *Y* units vertically from the last point you entered. Here's an example:

1. Select **Box** from the **Draw** menu.

2. First corner: Type r(1,1) ⏎.

    That's the *first* corner of a box; what's it relative *to?* The last point you entered, even if it was during a previous drawing operation. AutoSketch remembers the last point, even across different commands. In this case that was 8,5, so adding r(1,1) to it means that this point is at 9,6.

3. Second corner: type r(-5,-3) ⏎.

AutoSketch draws a box down and to the left from the first point. By typing r(-5,-3), you told AutoSketch to draw the box 5 units to the left (-5) and 3 units down (-3).

Polar coordinates

Remember the polar coordinates shown on the second coordinate display? You guessed it: the second method of entering coordinates is to use polar notation. Try it with a curve:

1. Select **Curve** from the **Draw** menu.

2. First point: Type 1,4⏎.

3. At the next few To point prompts, enter these polar coordinates:

   - p(1,315)⏎

   - p(2,45)⏎

   - p(2,315)⏎

   - Repeat the p(2,45),p(2,315) sequence twice more.

4. End the curve by typing /lpoint⏎.

Here's what you did:

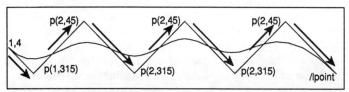

System variables

/lpoint is a *system variable*, used by AutoSketch to store the last point you entered. Remember that you terminate a curve by entering the last point twice; but, because you're using polar coordinates, you have no way of knowing the absolute position of the last point. Thus, /lpoint is the only way to find out the absolute position of that last point. There are other system variables, but they're pretty obscure; /lpoint is the one you'll use.

Visual Drawing Aids

Turning on the grid

AutoSketch has several on-screen "helpers" to assist you in creating precise drawings. The most obvious one is the grid. To turn on the grid, select **Grid** from the **Assist** menu (this is another toggled command). You could also press Alt+F6 to do this.

As soon as you turn on the grid, AutoSketch displays an array of dots. These dots are on the screen only; they don't appear in your drawing. The default spacing of the dots is 1 drawing unit; I'll show you how to change this *grid interval* later.

Snap mode

The grid helps you find locations visually, but by itself it still doesn't help you pick the exact location you want. Snap mode links the pointer to the grid. Turn on snap mode by selecting **Snap** from the **Assist** menu, or by pressing [Alt]+[F7].

With snap mode on, a small + (plus symbol) joins the pointer arrow on the screen. The pointer still moves freely, but the + symbol snaps from point to point, and shows the location of any points you pick. The default snap interval is also 1 drawing unit; that's why the pointer seems to snap to each grid dot.

The intervals between snap and grid points are based on the origin (0,0). For example, the default snap interval of 1 means that you can only pick points at multiples of 1 (for example: 0,0; 1,1; 8,-2; and so on). The pointer can't "fall into the cracks" between intervals.

You can change the snap interval and the grid interval separately; they don't have to be equal. Start by changing the snap interval:

Setting the snap interval

1. Select **Snap** from the **Settings** menu.

2. In the **Snap** dialog box, enter .5 into the **X Spacing** box, and then press [⏎].

    Notice that, as soon as you pressed [⏎], AutoSketch entered **.5** into the second box, **Y Spacing**. This is a convenience feature, since most of the time you'll want the X and Y intervals to be the same, although they don't have to be; you could enter a different value for Y spacing if you want.

3. Click **OK** to put away the dialog box.

After the dialog box disappears, AutoSketch redraws the grid using the new .5 interval. The pointer is now restricted to .5 intervals.

Setting the grid interval

By default, the grid interval is tied to the snap interval. As the snap interval gets smaller, the grid gets denser, so you might want to make the grid interval larger to clean up the display. Here's how:

1. Select **Grid** from the **Assist** menu.

   AutoSketch displays the **Grid** dialog box. Notice that the grid interval is set to **0**. A value of zero here is special; it tells AutoSketch to make the grid interval match the snap interval. When I said earlier that the grid interval defaults to 1, that was a simplification; in reality, the default grid interval of 0 ties the grid to the default snap interval of 1.

   Tying the grid to the snap interval

2. Enter 1 into the **X Spacing** box. After you press ⏎, AutoSketch copies 1 into the **Y Spacing** box.

3. Click **OK** to put away the dialog box.

AutoSketch again redraws the grid, this time at the original dot spacing of one drawing unit. Now the pointer snaps to the locations halfway between two dots, since its interval is still .5.

Use grid and snap intervals that are relevant to your drawing. For example, if you're designing a printed circuit board, you should use .1 as the snap interval (because electronic component pins are generally on 0.1 inch centers), with perhaps a grid interval of .5 so that the display isn't too cluttered by grid dots. An architectural drawing might require a snap interval of 2, since building supplies are generally some multiple of 2 inches in size (2x4-inch lumber, 4x8-foot plywood sheets, and so forth).

One advantage of snap mode is that you can more easily draw horizontal or vertical objects, or move or copy objects straight up or down or to the sides. Sometimes, though, you want to be *absolutely* sure of the horizontal and vertical. When it really matters, turn on AutoSketch's ortho mode.

1. Select **Ortho** from the **Assist** menu, or press Alt+F5.

   There's no immediate effect on pointer movement; you can still move it anywhere on the screen. Ortho only restricts actual operations.

   Ortho mode

2. Select **Line** from the **Draw** menu.

3. Pick the first point near the center of the screen.

4. Move the pointer around, and watch the rubberband line. With ortho on, you can draw only horizontal or vertical lines. AutoSketch simply ignores any other pointer positions.

The Attach Modes

Keyboard coordinate entry, and snap and ortho modes, go a long way toward your goal of precision drawing. AutoSketch's *ultimate* drawing aid is its attach mode, which works directly on objects in your drawing regardless of their coordinates.

Actually, the term *attach mode* doesn't do the feature justice. AutoSketch provides *eight* different attachment methods, each of which selects a different feature of objects. AutoSketch knows a lot of geometry, and because it stores your drawing as a database of geometrical objects, it knows a lot about each object in a drawing. Attach mode lets AutoSketch apply its knowledge of geometry to locate geometrical features of objects.

*Attach-
ment
methods*

A few examples will help you get the flavor of attach mode. The *endpoint* method finds the ends of lines, arcs, and curves, and the corners of boxes and polylines. Similarly, *midpoint* finds the exact middle of objects that have recognizable middles, such as lines and arcs. (AutoSketch can't find the middle of a circle since a circle has no beginning or end.) Use *center* to find the center of circles, arcs, and ellipses. The most useful of all may be the *intersect* attachment method, which finds the precise point at which two objects intersect. I use intersect-attach mode more than any other, primarily to locate points based on temporary lines; later in this Step I'll show you an example of that.

Start with the center attachment method to get the feel of it:

1. Turn off snap and ortho modes. A quick way to do this is to press Alt+F5, and then Alt+F7.

   Attach mode doesn't depend on snap or ortho, and they can often interfere with attach mode. Get into the habit of turning off snap and ortho when you're using attach mode.

2. Draw a circle in the center of the screen.

3. Select **Attach** from the Settings menu. AutoSketch displays the **Attachment Modes** dialog box, which looks like the sample to the right.

Attachment Modes	
Center	On
End Point	On
Intersect	On
Midpoint	On
Node Point	On
Perpendicular	On
Quadrant	On
Tangent	On
Attach Mode	Off

[OK] [Cancel]

Notice that you can use the **Attachment Modes** dialog box both to select a specific attachment method, and to turn on attach mode. This can be quite a convenience, because AutoSketch has so many attachment methods—you'll often find yourself changing methods as you work. Also, notice that, by default, *all* attachment methods are selected, and you generally want only one in particular. When you simply want to turn attach mode on or off, using the current attachment method, select **Attach** from the **Assist** menu or press [Alt]+[F8].

4. Click the pointer over each attach mode, except **Center**, to turn off the ones you won't be using now. As you click each mode, the word **Off** should appear next to it.

5. Click the word **Off** next to the legend **Attach Mode** to turn on attach mode. Click **OK** to put away the dialog box.

6. Select **Line** from the **Draw** menu.

7. Click the pointer on perimeter of the circle. *Bingo!* A rubberband line appears, anchored not where you clicked, but at the *center* of the circle. That's what center-attach mode does—it finds the exact geometrical center of a circle (or an arc or ellipse).

8. Select **Attach** from the **Settings** menu again. Turn off center, and turn on quadrant attachment method. Click **OK**.

9. Click on the perimeter of the circle again. AutoSketch draws the line from the center of the circle to the quadrant point nearest to where you click the pointer.

There are too many attach modes to describe them all here. A good way to learn them is to experiment. Here are a few suggestions:

- Use intersect-attach mode to find where a circle and a line intersect, by attaching another line to the intersection.

- Use quadrant-attach mode to find the four "corners" of a circle. Quadrants are the points located at 0°, 90°, 270°, and 360° around the circle.

- Try midpoint and endpoint to find the middle and ends of objects such as lines, arcs, and the edges of a box.

- Try out tangent-attach mode to attach a line *tangentially* to a circle or ellipse. This is harder to describe than use: the tangent point is where a line would touch a circle or ellipse at one point, and one point only. Note that a line that crosses a circle touches it at two points.

- Perpendicular-attach mode is like tangent-attach, except that it calculates where on a circle or ellipse to attach one end of a line so that the line leaves the object at a perpendicular (and, like tangent, it's easier to use than describe).

Power Drawing

The drawing aids described here help you create precise drawings with AutoSketch. With just a little practice, you'll learn to use each one, but fully mastering AutoSketch requires knowing which drawing aid to use in a given situation, and how to combine drawing aids to achieve maximum drawing power. You couldn't create the drawing on the next page without mastering AutoSketch's drawing aids (yes, it's correct; I intended it to be an optical illusion).

Using "scaf- foldings" for power drawing

The exercise that follows shows one philosophy of power drawing. This philosophy is to make lavish use of temporary objects (lines and circles) to create a "scaffolding" of guide lines, and then to use attach modes to draw objects precisely controlled by the scaffolding. When you're done you can "tear down the scaffolding" by erasing the objects that make it up, leaving behind a finished drawing.

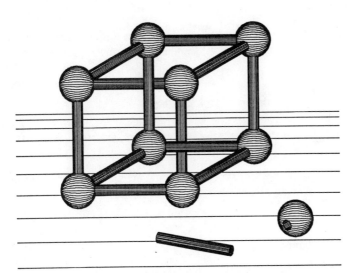

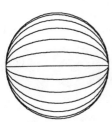

In this exercise you'll use a series of ellipses inside a circle to simulate the curvature of one of the balls (in other words, you'll be creating an optical illusion by making the ball look three-dimensional). It depends heavily on intersect-attach mode and on ortho mode. Exercises in later Steps will build on what you start here, so be sure to save the results in a file.

To keep things flowing, I'll use a compact notation to indicate the objects you should draw. For example, "Line; 0,4.5 to 14,4.5" means draw a line between those two points.

1. Clear out the current drawing with the **New** command on the **File** menu. Unless you want to save your attach mode experiments, click **Discard** in the **Save/Discard/Cancel** dialog box.

2. Turn on snap and ortho modes, and turn off attach. Set the snap interval to .5.

3. Line; 0,4.5 to 14,4.5

4. Line; 4,7 to 4,2

5. Line; 10,7 to 10,2

6. Circle; center at 4,4.5, radius = p(2,270)

7. Circle; center at 10,4.5, radius = p(2,270)

The result should look like this:

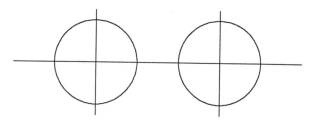

8. Turn off snap and ortho.

9. Select intersection-attach mode, turn all other attach modes off, and turn on attach mode. (Remember, you can do all that using just the **Attachment Modes** dialog box.)

10. Line; click at the intersection of the left vertical line and the horizontal line (intersect-attach mode finds the exact point); second point = p(2.5,15) (a 2.5-unit line at a 15° angle).

11. Line; from the circle center to p(2.5,30)

12. Line; from the circle center to p(2.5,45)

13. Line; from the circle center to p(2.5,60)

14. Line; from the circle center to p(2.5,75)

The result should look like this:

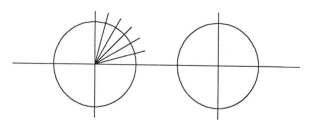

You're going to use the left circle with its radial lines, to create guidelines for the right circle. You'll project a series of lines to the right from the intersection of each radial with the circle, and then use these lines to determine where to put a series of ellipses in the right circle. The purpose of doing it this way is to use the ellipses to simulate the curvature of the ball. Because each radial intersects the circle at a hard-to-determine point, you can see how intersect-attach will save you a lot of time.

15. Turn ortho back on.

16. Line; click the pointer at the intersection of the first radial (at 15°) and the circle (intersect-attach mode does the hard part for you); draw the circle at least 6.3 drawing units to the right, so it extends beyond the circle on the right.

17. Draw four more horizontal guidelines from each of the radial/circle intersections to the right, passing through the circle on the right. The result should look like this:

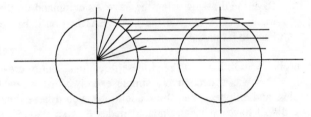

All five ellipses will have a common center (the intersection of the right vertical line and the horizontal line), and a common first-axis endpoint on the right (the intersection of the horizontal line with the right edge of the circle). Each ellipse's second-axis endpoint will be at the intersection of one of the horizontal guidelines you drew from the left circle radials and the right vertical line.

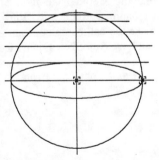

18. Ellipse; center and first axis endpoint as explained above; last endpoint at the intersection of the horizontal line projected from the 15° radial (the first guideline above the circle center) and the right vertical line.

19. Draw four more ellipses, each with a common center and common first-axis endpoint. Pick each ellipse's second-axis endpoint to match a different projected radial. The result should look like this:

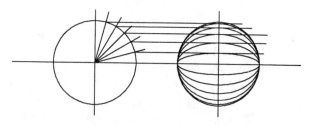

20. Save the drawing using the **Save As** command on the **File** menu. Give the file the name **BALL**; you'll be coming back to it later.

It probably took longer to read these directions than to create the ball. This was a deceptively simple exercise; just a few lines, circles, and ellipses. Yet, think about how you'd have done it if you didn't have ortho and attach modes at your service. This drawing would have required performing some fairly intricate trigonometry on a calculator, and a lot of just plain "fudging" to make the ball come out right. Why do it the hard way, when you can have AutoSketch do all the work for you?

Now *that's* power drawing!

No drawing or CAD program would be complete without tools to modify a drawing. AutoSketch has such a rich set of "change" tools that I need two steps to cover them properly. In this Step you'll learn about the basic change tools: copy, move, and erase; how to pick objects to change; and the undo/redo safety net.

Picking Objects

Before you can change an object in your drawing, you must select it using one of three methods.

Point and Click Picking

The direct way to pick an object for changing is to click on it with the pointer. If AutoSketch finds an object near the pointer, it selects it; otherwise, AutoSketch assumes that you want to use a selection box (described next).

If there are several objects near the pointer, AutoSketch selects the most recently drawn object. If attach mode is turned on, it has priority: an object that satisfies the selected attachment method is selected over other objects that don't satisfy it.

Picking Objects with a Selection Box

When you click the pointer in an empty area of your drawing, AutoSketch assumes that you want to use a *selection box*. You define a selection box the same way you draw a box: the first point defines one corner, and the second point defines the second corner of the selection box.

AutoSketch has two kinds of selection boxes. The one it uses is determined by the direction you move the pointer away from the first point.

*Window
selection
boxes*

If you move the pointer to the *right* after defining the first point of a selection box, you define a window selection box. AutoSketch selects only objects that are *entirely within* the selection box.

*Crosses
selection
box*

If you move the pointer to the *left*, you define a crosses selection box. AutoSketch selects *all objects that the box crosses;* the box need only touch an object for it to be included in the selection.

Erasing Objects, and Undo/Redo

The most basic change command is **Erase**. Use **Erase** now to exercise the different methods of picking objects:

1. Select **Open** from the **File** menu, and load **ENGINE**. (Don't save the drawing while you work.)

2. Select **Erase** from the **Change** menu.

3. Practice erasing by directly picking some of the objects in the drawing. Stay away from the cab of the engine; you'll be working with it next.

4. Practice picking objects with a window selection box. Start by picking a point in the empty area below and to the left of the window in the cab (see Figure 8.1). Use the **Zoom Box** command if you can't see the cab area clearly.

   AutoSketch erases all the objects that were totally enclosed by the selection box. Figure 8.1 shows these objects as dotted lines.

*The
Undo
command*

5. Select **Undo** from the **Change** menu.

   AutoSketch restores the objects you erased. **Undo** is your safety net: you can change your mind and reverse any drawing or editing operation. It also lets you experiment, since the things you try don't have to be permanent.

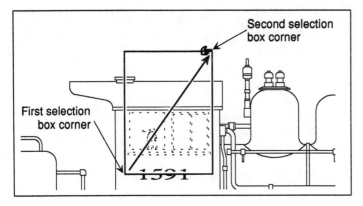

Figure 8.1: Erasing with a window selection box

6. Select **Redo** from the **Change** menu.

   AutoSketch again erases the objects you selected. **Redo** is sort of an "undo-undo" command; you can use it to reinstate changes you reversed with **Undo**.

7. Select **Undo** again; you'll be experimenting some more on those erased objects.

8. This time, use a crosses selection box to erase some objects. Start the box to the right of, and below, the cab window, as shown in Figure 8.2. Draw the box up and to the left, and click when the box encloses the window.

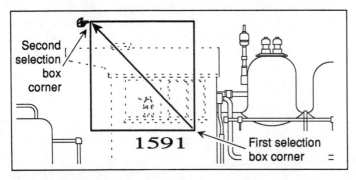

Figure 8.2: Erasing with a crosses selection box

This time, AutoSketch erases all the objects that touched the selection box; these are shown with dotted lines in Figure 8.2.

Moving Objects

1. Select **New** from the **File** menu; discard the changes to the current drawing.

2. Draw a box somewhere on the screen.

3. Select **Move** from the **Change** menu.

4. Click on the box.

5. From point: Pick a point about an inch from the box.

   This first point is a reference point for the move. Its relationship to the next point determines the distance and direction in which AutoSketch moves the selected object.

6. To point: Click the pointer at a new location. AutoSketch erases the box at its original location and redraws it at the new location.

Copying Objects

You copy an object (or objects) in exactly the same way as you move objects. All of the prompts, and the actions you take in response to them, are exactly the same as when you use the **Move** command. What's different is the result: AutoSketch doesn't erase the object at its original location. Instead, it draws a copy of the selected object or objects at the new location. Select **Copy** from the **Change** menu and try it.

Advanced Change Skills

The basic change tools you learned about in the last Step make major modifications to a drawing (moving, copying, or erasing objects). The advanced change tools have more subtle uses: they're "surgical" tools that let you change the appearance of objects. As part of your power drawing toolbox, these tools are a way to create new objects from the basic drawing objects—for example, elliptical arcs created by breaking an ellipse into pieces.

The exercise in this Step is another part of the optical illusion cube from Step 7: the rod linking the ball. This drawing will be based on the **BALL** drawing you started in that Step, so you must first make a copy of this drawing called **ROD**:

1. Use the **Open** command on the **File** menu to load the **BALL** drawing.

2. Use the **Save As** command from the **File** menu to save the drawing under the new name **ROD**.

3. Use a window selection box to erase the ball and its component ellipses. Leave behind the guideline scaffolding like this:

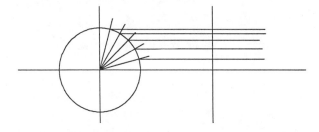

Stretching an Object

The **Stretch** command elongates objects. Use it now to extend the horizontal guidelines (they'll make up part of the rod).

1. Scroll the display right by clicking in the right half of the bottom scroll bar.

2. Select **Stretch** from the **Change** menu, or use the F7 function key shortcut.

   This command requires you to select one or more *control points* on an object to stretch, rather than selecting the object itself. Control points are the points that define an object (for example, line endpoints, box corners, and so on). You use a special selection box with **Stretch**; it's always a window selection box (a selection box that captures only the control points within the box), and it doesn't matter whether you draw it to the left or right.

3. Stretch First Corner: Draw a selection box to capture the right endpoints of all six horizontal guidelines:

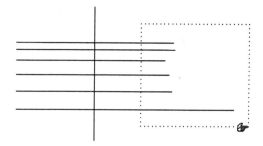

4. When the selection box encompasses all the endpoints, click the pointer.

5. Stretch base: This is a reference point just like the base point used with the **Copy** and **Move** commands. Position this point above the endpoints, at approximately 11,7.

6. Stretch to: p(7,0) ⏎ (stretch the lines 7 drawing units to the right).

   AutoSketch redraws the five guidelines, extended by the distance between the "stretch base" and the "stretch to" point.

The **BALL** drawing didn't have a guideline at the top of the left circle. Use **Zoom Full** to make all of the drawing visible, and add a line now that extends roughly as far as the other five guidelines. (Refer back to Step 7 if you don't remember how you did it then.) The drawing, including the new top line, looks like this:

Breaking Objects

One of the most useful **Change** menu commands is **Break**. **Break** is your "scalpel"—you use it to cut objects into pieces. The general technique is to pick two *break points* that specify where AutoSketch is to break the object. You can pick these points in several ways to control the kind of surgery you perform.

We'll start with a simple exercise: breaking the horizontal lines to exactly meet two ellipses that represent the ends of the rod.

1. Make sure that ortho and attach modes are off, and turn on snap mode. The snap interval should be set to .5, which is the snap interval AutoSketch saved with the file.

2. Ellipse   Center of ellipse: 9.5,4.5
                     Axis endpoint: 10.5,4.5
                     Other axis distance: 9.5,6.5

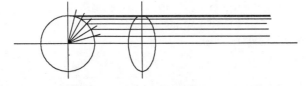

3. Turn off snap mode. Select the intersection-attach method, and turn on attach mode.

4. Use **Zoom Box** on the **View** menu to zoom in to the area of the upper half of the ellipse (similar to the region shown to the right).

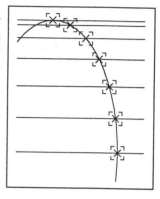

5. Select the **Break** command from the **Change** menu, or press F4.

6. `Select object:` Pick the top horizontal line. Auto-Sketch highlights the line you selected.

7. `First break point:` Pick a location close to the intersection of the line and the right edge of the ellipse (intersection-attach will find the exact point for you). The figure above shows the first break points for each line.

8. `Second break point:` Pick a point somewhere to the left beyond the ellipse. The exact location isn't important.

9. Repeat these steps to truncate each of the lines flush with the ellipse. The drawing should look like this:

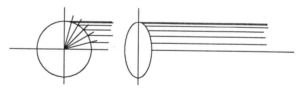

You've seen that AutoSketch removes the portion of an object between the two break points. You can also put both break points at the same location to break an object into two pieces without removing anything:

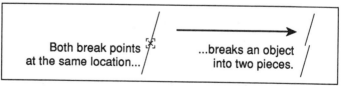

Both break points at the same location... ...breaks an object into two pieces.

You can put the second break point beyond the end of an object to truncate it back to the first break point:

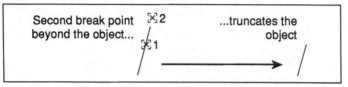

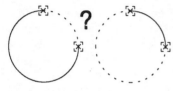

The meaning of the two break points is obvious for open-ended objects like lines, but what do the two points mean on a closed object like a circle? The piece to be cut out could lie between the two points in either a clockwise or counter-clockwise direction. To solve this problem, the designers of AutoSketch chose to remove the piece counter-clockwise from the first point to the second. Here's how it works on an ellipse:

1. Use the **Zoom Full** command to view all of the drawing.

2. Draw a vertical line from 17.5,2.5 that's 4.5 units tall. Enter 17.5,2.5 using the keyboard, or turn on snap mode to locate this point. You can enter the second point as p(4.5,90).

3. Turn on endpoint-attach mode in addition to intersection-attach. In this situation you'll use both in combination.

4. Copy the ellipse 7 drawing units to the right. Because endpoint-attach mode is turned on, you can pick the base point at the end of the top line (where it meets the ellipse); and because intersection-attach mode is also turned on, you can pick the "to point" at the intersection of the vertical line you drew earlier with the top horizontal line.

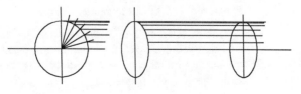

5. Use the **Zoom Box** command to zoom in to the region around the right ellipse.

6. Select the **Break** command again, and select the ellipse.

7. Pick the first break point at the intersection of the top of the ellipse with the vertical guideline. Pick the second break point at the intersection of the bottom of the ellipse with the vertical line.

The order in which you picked the break points ensured that AutoSketch leaves behind the right half of the ellipse, which is the edge of the rod. To finish, turn off endpoint-attach, and break each of the horizontal lines where they intersect this elliptical arc; place the second break point beyond the end of each line to truncate them. Erase both vertical lines, and the rest of the scaffolding. The results should look like this:

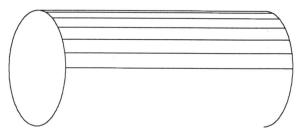

Mirroring Objects

You now have half a cylinder. You could finish it the hard way by drawing more lines for the bottom half...or you could do it the smart way and use the **Mirror** command to make a mirror image copy of the top half at the bottom.

1. Turn endpoint-attach on, and intersection-attach off.

2. Select **Mirror** from the **Change** menu or press Ctrl+F3.

3. Use a crosses selection box to pick the top six horizontal lines; be sure you don't pick the center line, or either ellipse. (If you do this by mistake, simply select **Mirror** again to cancel the previous operation.)

4. `Base point:` Pick the left end of the center line (that's easy with endpoint-attach turned on).

5. `Second point:` Pick the other end of the center line.

Mirroring reflects the selected objects across a *mirror line*. In this case the mirror line is the center line, and the mirrored copy will end up below the center line. After you pick the second point, AutoSketch mirrors the selected lines below the center line. The results should look like this:

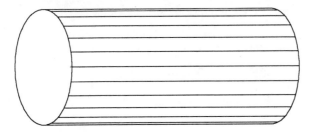

Scaling Objects

The rod you've drawn is the same size as the ball you drew earlier, since you used the same guidelines. Use the **Scale** command to make it 50% smaller.

1. Select **Scale** from the **Change** menu, or press Ctrl + F6.

2. `Select object:` Use a window selection box to select all the lines and both ellipses.

3. `Base point:` Pick a point in the middle of the left ellipse. This point provides a reference only, so its exact location doesn't matter.

4. `Second point:` Move the pointer away from the base point. Watch the prompt line; AutoSketch displays the scale of the objects there. Move the pointer until the scale is .5—that's 50%—and then click. AutoSketch redraws the rod at the new scale.

Rotating Objects

If you refer to the cube illustration in Step 7, you see that the cube is made up of horizontal rods as well as rods at a 20° angle. Use the **Rotate** command to rotate a copy of the rod.

1. Make a copy of the rod in the empty area of your drawing.

2. Select **Rotate** from the **Change** menu, or press Ctrl+F5.

3. Select object: Use a window selection box to select the entire rod (either the original or the copy).

4. Center of rotation: Pick the left end of the center line (this means that you'll pivot the rod around this point).

5. As you move the pointer away from the center point, AutoSketch displays an outline of the rod, and displays rotation in the prompt line. You can rotate the rod 20° in either of two ways:

    *   Watch the rotation angle as shown in the prompt line, and click when the rotation is 20°.

    *   Use the keyboard to enter the rotation directly as a polar coordinate. For example, enter p(5,20)↵. Note that the distance you enter doesn't matter, just the bearing.

    Your drawing should look like this:

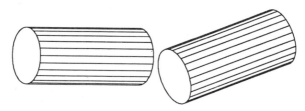

You're done with the **ROD** drawing for now, so save it by selecting **New** from the **File** menu, and tell AutoSketch to save your changes. (This shortcut uses the **Save/Discard/Cancel** dialog box to combine starting a new drawing with saving the current one.)

Chamfers and Fillets

Chamfers and fillets are AutoSketch's "sandpaper"—they're two ways to round off or bevel the corner between two lines, the corner of a box, or the junction between two polyline segments. (I'll be explaining polylines in Step 12.) This illustration shows the effect of both these commands.

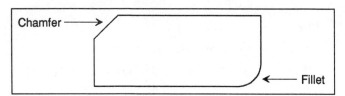

In both cases you pick two intersecting objects (lines or two adjacent sides of a box, for example), and AutoSketch chamfers or fillets. You control how far back from the intersection the chamfer or fillet starts with the **Settings** menu:

- For chamfers, you set the distance back from the intersection point individually for the first and second objects you pick. This means that the chamfer line connecting the two objects doesn't have to be symmetrical. The default values are both .5 drawing units.

- For fillets, you set a single value, the fillet radius. This is the radius of the arc that connects the two objects. The default radius is .5 drawing units.

Chamfering

1. Draw a box in the middle of the screen.

2. Select **Chamfer** from the **Settings** menu. Set the first chamfer distance to 1, and the second to .5.

3. Select **Chamfer** from the **Change** menu.

4. Select object(s): Pick the top left edge of the box. The prompt is this way because you could use a crosses selection box to pick two objects at once.

5. `Select second segment:` Pick the right edge of the box.

AutoSketch redraws the box with the chamfer added to the upper right corner. Because you set the two chamfer distances to be different, you can see how the order in which you pick the objects affects the appearance of the chamfer.

Filleting

1. Select **Fillet** from the **Change** menu.

2. This time, use a crosses selection box to pick both the bottom edge and the left edge of the box.

As soon as you've selected both edges, AutoSketch redraws the box with a fillet arc inserted into the lower left corner.

Zero-Size Chamfers and Fillets

An interesting wrinkle to both chamfers and fillets is that if you set the chamfer distances to 0, or the fillet radius to 0, you can use either command to precisely join two existing objects. The only requirement is that the two objects would intersect if they were projected to their common point. Here's how this works.

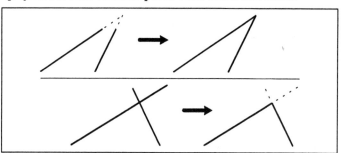

Grouping Objects

Remember, in the previous steps when you were trying to select an entire collection of objects like the ball or the rod, how you had to use a selection box and carefully select just the objects you wanted? A little miscalculation, and you'd have either missed some of the objects or picked up others you didn't want. AutoSketch's **Group** command lets you *group* objects together so that you can pick them as if they were a single object. Naturally, there's an **Ungroup** command to separate the group into its component objects.

In these exercises you'll be using the **ROD** drawing again, so load it into AutoSketch with the **Open** command.

The Group Command

1. Select **Group** from the **Change** menu, or press Alt+F10.

2. Use a selection box (your choice: a crosses box drawn to the left, or a window box drawn to the right) to select all the objects that make up the rotated rod. After you've drawn the selection box, AutoSketch highlights all the objects in the rod.

3. Select the **Group** command again to finish grouping objects. AutoSketch redraws them.

The reason you had to explicitly tell AutoSketch when you're done is that you can repeatedly pick objects to add to a group; you don't have to capture them all at once. Try it out now:

1. Use a crosses selection box to pick just the horizontal lines in the unrotated rod. (**Group** is still selected.) Notice that only the lines are highlighted.

2. Pick each ellipse at the ends of the rod. As you do, each one is highlighted to show you that it's been added to the group.

3. Select the **Group** command again to signal that you're done.

4. Verify that each rod is now a group by moving each one individually. You can pick a whole rod by just clicking the pointer anywhere on it.

Ungrouping Objects

Immediately after using the **Group** command, you can separate the group into its components by using **Undo**. Later, after using other commands, you have to use the **Ungroup** command.

1. Select **Ungroup** from the **Change** menu.

2. Click the pointer on either rod (you don't have to use a selection box since groups are single objects for most purposes). AutoSketch immediately redraws the rod.

3. Verify that the rod has been separated into individual objects by erasing or moving a single line or ellipse. Be sure to use **Undo** to restore the rod to its original state. If you use **Undo** enough times you'll also recreate the group (in other words, you'll reverse the **Ungroup** command).

4. Save the drawing.

Restrictions on Groups

You can't have more than 1000 objects in a group, but you can have groups within groups. This is called *nesting* groups, and you can nest groups up to eight levels deep. A group can be part of a larger group, which in turn is part of yet another group, and another...something like little fish being swallowed by ever-larger fish, up to eight fish (as long as the fish are groupers).

Some **Change** menu commands don't work on groups, or they have limitations. You can't break objects in a group, and you can't stretch an entire group, unless the group consists of only one type of object and you select a part of each object to stretch. You can, however, erase, move, copy, array, rotate, scale, and mirror groups just like single objects.

Properties of Objects

So far you've drawn most objects using their default properties. When you drew text in Step 6, you learned that you could select different text properties such as height, angle, and so on. In fact, all objects have at least two basic properties—color and layer— and most objects have other properties as well.

Color

AutoSketch stores an object's color in the object database as a number from 1 through 127. That's all AutoSketch knows about color. The color you see on your display or on your plotted drawing depends on how the output device interprets the color number.

The first seven color numbers have been assigned standard names that you see when you select **Color** from the **Settings** menu and display the **Drawing Color** dialog box:

Standard colors

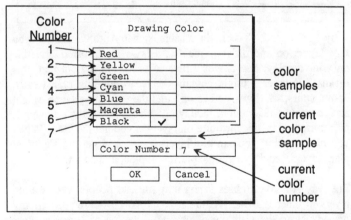

You select the current color by clicking on one of the predefined color names or typing a number from 1 to 127 into the **Color Number** box. The meaning of color numbers greater than 7 depends on how your display, plotter, or printer interprets the number.

Device-dependent colors

Even if you can't plot/print a drawing in color, it's worthwhile to use color while you work (if you have a color display) to make objects stand out from one another, to group related objects visually, and to identify layers by color.

Layers

You can assign an object to any one of 10 layers. Using layers in AutoSketch is a lot like using several sheets of clear plastic film, stacked one on top of the other, each containing part of your drawing, like this floorplan:

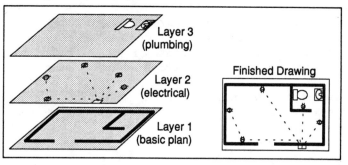

Layer 3
(plumbing)

Layer 2
(electrical)

Layer 1
(basic plan)

Finished Drawing

Why use layers? The main reason is that AutoSketch lets you turn layers on and off individually; a layer that's off is invisible on your display, and it won't plot or print. In a floorplan, this means that layer 1 might contain the basic building plan (walls, doors, stairs, windows, and so on), and the remaining layers might each contain one aspect of the layout: electrical wiring on layer 2, plumbing on layer 3, furniture on layer 4...you get the idea. When you plot or print, you can plot layers 1 and 2 to get the electrical plan, layers 1 and 3 to get the plumbing plan, and so on.

The way AutoSketch uses layers may mislead people who've used layers in other drawing programs: AutoSketch doesn't assign any precedence to the visibility of objects according to layer, as other programs do. That is, objects on layer 2 are not on top of layer 1; rather, object precedence is determined by the order in which you draw objects. This makes no difference for black and white drawings—you can't tell what's on top of what anyway—but if you use color, the order in which you draw objects determines which one is obscured when two objects overlap.

Layer visibility, and the current layer, are controlled by the **Layer Status** dialog box, available from the **Layer** command on the **Settings** menu (see the example to the right). Click on the appropriate box in the first column to select the current layer; click on the appropriate boxes in the second column to select the visible layers.

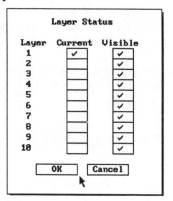

More Properties than a Real Estate Agent

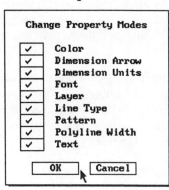

AutoSketch deals with a lot of properties that apply to individual objects or to categories of objects. If you select **Property** from the **Settings** menu, Auto-Sketch displays a dialog box like the example to the left showing you the properties you can change. (I'll explain what this dialog box is for later.)

After color and layer, the most universal property is line type. It controls how all zero-width lines are drawn, as shown here:

Line type

Solid	——————	· · · · · · · · · ·	Dot
Dashed	– — — — —	— · — · — · –	Dashdot
Hidden	--------------	— · — · —	Border
Center	——— – ———	· · — · · —	Divide
Phantom	——— – – ———	································	Dots

Zero-
width
lines

What's a zero-width line? It's simply a line plotted or printed at the finest resolution your output device provides: the width of a pen tip on a plotter or the size of a single dot on a printer. The only kind of lines that aren't zero-width are polylines, which, not so coincidentally, are the subject of the next Step.

I won't try to explain here each of the properties you can control; rather, I'll describe each one when I introduce the object to which it applies.

Changing Properties

AutoSketch draws each object with the properties in effect at the time you draw the object. Naturally, AutoSketch lets you change the properties of objects after the fact.

AutoSketch's method for changing properties is subtle and powerful. It's a two-step process: first, select the properties you want to change in the **Change Property Modes** dialog box (**Property** on the **Settings** menu), and then change the properties (select **Property** from the **Change** menu, and pick the objects whose properties you want to change).

Selecting
properties
to change

What makes it subtle is your ability to selectively change properties. The **Change Property Modes** dialog box acts as a filter—only those properties checked (turned on) in this dialog box get changed. That means that, for example, you can change the color of a line without disturbing its layer or line type.

Naturally, you can only change appropriate properties. If you try to change the line type of text, nothing happens.

Text
properties

Speaking of text, notice that the **Change Property Modes** dialog box has both a **Font** selection and a **Text** selection. **Font** changes only the font of selected text, while **Text** changes all the other text properties, such as height, angle, and so on. This is handy when you want to change the font of all text in a drawing without disturbing the other characteristics of the text.

A *polyline* is a sequence of connected straight line and arc segments. AutoSketch treats a polyline as a single object for **Change** menu operations. Sure, you could do the same thing by grouping a lot of individual lines and arcs, but the payoff is that you can control the width of a polyline. If a polyline has a non-zero width, you can also control whether its interior is empty or solid, or even filled with a pattern. You'll first learn how to draw zero-width polylines, and then move on to wide polylines.

Drawing Polylines

Let's start with a polyline consisting of just straight line segments (that's the default mode). If the display isn't clean, use **New** from the **File** menu to start fresh.

1. Select **Polyline** from the **Draw** menu, or press Ctrl+F2.

2. Respond in the usual way to the First point prompt.

   (By now you should understand the mechanics of drawing objects, and I'll try to avoid needless repetition from now on.)

3. After the first point, AutoSketch will continue to prompt you for points. Each point marks one junction, or *vertex*, between consecutive line segments in the polyline. Pick several points.

4. Double-click the last point; this tells AutoSketch that you're done with the polyline.

This is an *open* polyline since the last point is different from the first. You can create a *closed* polyline by picking the last point at the same location as the first point (doing this also terminates the polyline).

Now, let's move on to inserting arc segments within polylines.

*Arc
mode*

1. Start another polyline.

2. At one of the prompts asking for another point, press [Ctrl]+[F1] to switch to arc mode. (There's also an **Assist** menu **Arc Mode** command, but this is one of those situations where the keyboard shortcut is more convenient.)

3. Drawing in arc mode is just like drawing a single arc. The last vertex marks the first point of the arc. Now supply the `Point on arc` and the `Arc segment endpoint`.

4. Press [Ctrl]+[F1] again to toggle back to line-segment drawing, and draw a few more line segments.

   You could also remain in arc mode to draw a sequence of several arcs.

5. Terminate the polyline by double-clicking the final point.

If you start a polyline and the first prompt you see is `Arc segment start point`, you'll know that you left arc mode turned on during the last polyline operation. If you intended to start with a line segment, just toggle arc mode. You should get into the habit of checking the prompt line when you start a polyline to see whether arc mode is turned on.

Wide Polylines

Wide polylines can be very useful. Earlier versions of AutoSketch didn't have polylines at all, but once you've used wide polylines, you'll wonder how you could have managed without them. If you're designing a printed circuit board, wide polylines make painless traces. If you're working on a floorplan, wide polylines make drawing the walls a snap. In many situations wide lines add emphasis; for example you can make the borders of boxes in a chart stand out from the other lines.

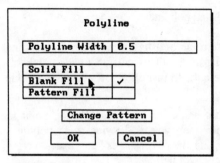

The technique for drawing wide polylines is the same as for zero-width polylines. The difference is that you first set the width by selecting **Polyline** from the **Settings** menu to display the **Polyline** dialog box (see the example above). The buttons and boxes on this dialog box do the following:

Polyline Width   Is obvious: enter the width of the polyline in drawing units. Note that AutoSketch draws the polyline *centered* around the vertices; half the width will end up on each side of the vertex.

Solid Fill   Draws the polyline with a solid interior in the current color.

Blank Fill   Draws polylines with an empty interior and solid borders; the interior is transparent and objects behind the polyline will be visible. This is useful for things like walls in a floorplan.

Pattern Fill   Draws the polyline interior filled with the current pattern (see comments below.)

Change Pattern   Displays the **Pattern Settings** dialog box so that you can select a new pattern (see comments below).

The first three boxes are straightforward, but what are these *patterns* in the last two boxes? Patterns are another new AutoSketch feature: the ability to draw pattern-filled objects. I can't describe patterns first, because you draw patterns using the same technique as polylines (a real "chicken-and-the-egg" problem). Patterns are the subject of the next Step, so for now take it on faith, and I'll return to pattern-filled polylines in that Step.

Let's draw a wide solid-filled polyline.

1. Select **Polyline** from the **Settings** menu. Set the polyline width to .5 drawing units. (This will be a *wide* polyline!) Solid fill is the default, so just click **OK** to put away this dialog box.

2. Turn snap on. It's harder to find your starting point to finish the polyline when you're drawing wide polylines because the polyline itself obscures the exact vertex location. Snap mode will help.

3. Draw a polyline as before, using a combination of line and arc segments.

Notice that the rubberband line (which now shows an approximation of the wide polyline) behaves differently. After the first point, it acts like a line rubberband. After the second point, the first segment is still an outline. It's only after the third point that AutoSketch begins to fill in the polyline, and fill continues to lag one segment behind for the rest of the polyline. It works this way because AutoSketch needs to see the angle at which two segments meet at a vertex before it knows how to draw their junction (more on these junctions later).

Power Polylines

This section deals with the subtleties of polylines and gives you a way to work around a problem in AutoSketch Version 3.0.

Limitations on Polylines

A polyline can have no more than 200 vertices, including the first and last points. Only vertices count toward this limit; if your polyline includes arcs, the "point on arc" (the middle point) doesn't count. If you reach the limit, AutoSketch displays an error message and ends the polyline with the last point you entered. You may be able to continue with another polyline, or you might have to rethink your polyline. You may have trouble matching the junction of two wide polylines since AutoSketch won't be able to miter them.

The Wide Polyline "Bug"

Well, not a bug exactly, but this problem surfaced late in the development cycle and the programmers weren't able to find a clean way to improve it. (Autodesk, to it's credit, hates to "kludge" and patch things, and so decided it was better to not disturb a part of the program that in every other way works beautifully.) We developed this work-around too late to get it into the manuals, so here it is—an *Up & Running with AutoSketch 3* exclusive!

AutoSketch has trouble joining the boundary lines between arc and straight segments of blank and pattern-filled wide polylines (solid polylines also, but the problem is invisible). It looks like this:

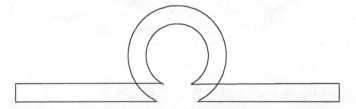

You can improve the appearance of these junctions after the fact by filleting them. You're limited to filleting at no smaller than one-half the width of the polyline (any smaller would be mathematically impossible), but at least you can smooth out the junction. The previous example would look like this, after applying a 0.25 radius fillet to the 0.5-unit wide polyline:

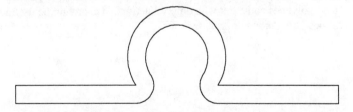

One consequence of this problem is that if your wide polyline must include arcs, it may be better to first draw the polyline with line segments only, and then fillet the polyline where necessary to add arcs. This only works with arcs that span less than 180°.

Mitering Polylines

On a more positive note, here's something to be aware of that isn't a problem.   When AutoSketch draws the junction of two polyline segments at a vertex, it must decide the style of the junction (the *miter* at the junction).   That is, whether to bring the segments together in a point, or to bevel the junction.   The decision-point is 28°; segments that meet at an angle greater than this are drawn meeting in a point, while segments meeting at less than 28° are squared-off, like this:

Displaying and Plotting Wide Polylines

Sometimes the presence of wide solid or pattern-filled polylines slows down AutoSketch when it's redrawing the display.   To speed things up, turn off **Fill** on the **Assist** menu, and AutoSketch will display these polylines with empty interiors (whatever fill you specified when you drew the polyline won't be displayed).

Fill also affects plotting/printing: with fill off, wide, solid, or pattern-filled polylines come out with empty interiors. This might be useful to speed up plotting or printing drafts.

Step 13

Patterns

Now that you know how to draw polylines, you can draw pattern-filled objects just as easily. (I'll just call them "pattern fills" from now on.) For the purposes of creating it, you can consider a pattern fill to be a closed polyline whose interior is filled with one of dozens of built-in patterns. These are the elements of a pattern fill:

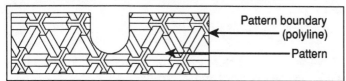

Pattern boundary
(polyline)

Pattern

That really interesting pattern, by the way, is called **ESCHER**, in honor of Dutch artist M.C. Escher, whose 1952 lithograph *Cubic Space-Division* inspired this pattern and generations of playful draftspersons. It doesn't have too many practical applications, but it's sure fun to use.

Drawing Patterns

The process is just like drawing a polyline, except:

1. Select **Pattern Fill** from the **Draw** menu. Draw the pattern fill as if you're drawing a closed polyline.

2. After you picked the last point, AutoSketch fills in the boundary with the default pattern, called **CRSSHTCH** (cross-hatch), and displays a small dialog box with two buttons: **Accept** and **Modify**. For now click **Accept**; I'll deal with **Modify** when we look at how you select different patterns.

AutoSketch draws the pattern fill as a series of lines. It's an indivisible unit: you can't ungroup it and edit individual lines in the pattern. I told you to draw a closed polyline, but you don't have to. If the last point isn't the same as the first, AutoSketch simply adds one more line connecting the first and last points, and that line becomes the last segment of the boundary.

You can allow two boundary segments cross each other without confusing AutoSketch. It knows when it's "inside" or "outside" a pattern fill. Here's an example of what I mean:

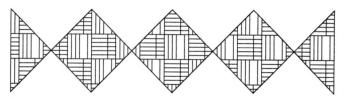

Selecting Patterns

AutoSketch creates each pattern from a script stored in files with a **.PAT** extension; the first part of the file name is the same as the name of the pattern. This explains why the **Pattern Settings** dialog box contains icons like other file selection dialog boxes, and why pattern names are limited to eight characters, like **CRSSHTCH**—AutoSketch manages patterns like it manages files. The dialog box looks like Figure 13.1.

To pick the pattern with which you'll draw your next pattern fill:

1. Select **Pattern** from the **Settings** menu.

2. In the dialog box, click on the icon representing the pattern you want. Use the scroll bar at the right to see the rest of the list of patterns. After you click an icon, its name appears in the **Active Pattern** box. You could also select from a list of pattern names; if you click the **Names** box, AutoSketch replaces the icon-style dialog box with a name-list dialog box.

3. Click **OK** to put away the dialog box.

This method determines how future pattern fills are drawn. There's another, interactive, way of controlling patterns while you draw a pattern fill. Remember the dialog box with **Accept** and **Modify** buttons that appears when you finish a pattern boundary? If you click **Modify**, AutoSketch displays the **Pattern Settings** dialog box so that you can modify pattern settings. You can "loop" between the **Accept/Modify** dialog box and the **Pattern**

Settings dialog box as many times as you want until the pattern fill is set the way you want it.

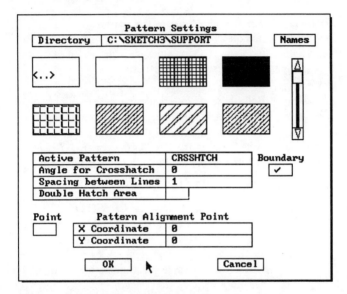

Figure 13.1: The Pattern Selection dialog box

You can also change an existing pattern fill using the **Property** command on the **Change** menu in conjunction with the **Settings** menu **Property** command property filter. You must pick a pattern fill by clicking on one of its edges; clicking in the center won't do it.

The sample **Pattern Settings** dialog box shown previously shows the options for **CRSSHTCH** only. When you select other patterns, the middle set of options changes to:

Active Pattern	ANSI32	Boundary
Angle for Pattern	0	✓
Scale for Pattern	0.025	

All of these settings control the appearance of patterns. Here's what they do:

Rotating a pattern

Angle for Crosshatch or Angle for Pattern　These options rotate the pattern. Zero means that the pattern is drawn exactly as it appears in the icon. Other values shift the angle of all the lines that make up a pattern.

Sizing a pattern

Spacing Between Lines or Scale for Pattern　Both these options scale the pattern. If the pattern is **CRSSHTCH**, the **Spacing Between Lines** directly specifies the distance in drawing units between the lines in the pattern. For other patterns, **Scale for Pattern** specifies a factor that scales the entire pattern uniformly.

Double Hatch Area　This box appears only for **CRSSHTCH**. When this box is checked (the default), AutoSketch draws an array of both horizontal and vertical lines (or two sets of lines at right angles to each other, rotated by the **Angle for Crosshatch** setting). If you turn it off, the pattern consists only of horizontal lines (or a single set of lines rotated by the **Angle for Crosshatch** setting).

Pattern origin

Point, X Coordinate, and Y Coordinate　AutoSketch draws patterns from a script, and by default, it starts the pattern at 0,0. You can change the origin of the pattern using these settings. **Point** unchecked means that you type the coordinates into the other two boxes. **Point** checked lets you click the pointer to specify the pattern origin.

Boundary　When this box is checked (the default), the pattern fill includes a boundary. You can turn off the boundary and draw just the pattern by clicking this button.

Experiment with some of the pattern settings now. (I won't go into changing the pattern origin; it's unlikely that you'll ever need to change it.)

1. Draw a pattern fill. Click **Modify** to display the **Pattern Settings** dialog box.

2. Make **ESCHER** the active pattern (you'll have to scroll down the list to find it), set the pattern angle to 45 (45°), and the pattern scale to .5. Click **OK** to have AutoSketch redraw the pattern fill with these new settings.

3. Select **Scale** from the **Change** menu, and make the pattern fill larger (values greater than 1) or smaller (values less than 1).

That last step illustrated an important point about pattern fills: the scale of the pattern itself is controlled only by the **Scale for Pattern** box in the **Pattern Settings** dialog box. Using the **Scale** command on the pattern fill only changes the size of the boundary, and the pattern in the interior remains at the scale specified by **Scale for Pattern**.

Pattern-Filled Wide Polylines

I promised in the last Step to explain this, but by now it will be an anticlimax. You simply draw a wide polyline in the current pattern:

1. Select **Polyline** from the **Settings** menu. Give the polyline a non-zero width (try .5 for this example), and click **Pattern Fill**. You could also click **Change Pattern** to select another pattern, but for now let's stick with **ESCHER**.

2. Draw the polyline.

The only difference with wide polylines is that the **Boundary** checkbox has no effect. Wide pattern-filled polylines always have a boundary.

Pattern Power

Here's a collection of power tips for using AutoSketch patterns.

Pattern Transparency

AutoSketch patterns are transparent; that is, if you draw a pattern on top of another pattern, the bottom pattern shows through. You can't do this...

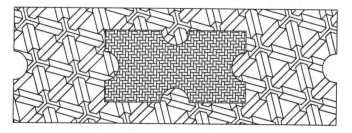

...because it will turn out looking like this:

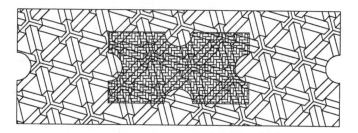

But the first illustration looks like I *did* what I said you *couldn't* do! What's the secret? You cheat: draw "hollow" patterns, so that the patterns don't actually overlap. If you have to join two patterns together to look like a single pattern, draw them without borders, and overlay a polyline to provide the overall border. Because the patterns start at a common origin (the pattern alignment point), they'll mesh as if they're the same pattern.

Here's an exploded view that reveals my secrets:

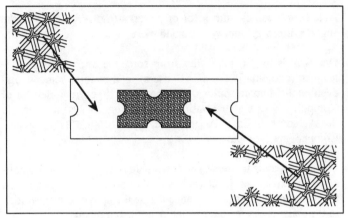

Pattern Display and Printing

AutoSketch may take a long time to redraw the screen if you have a lot of pattern fills in a drawing. Luckily, **Fill** on the **Assist** menu has the same effect on patterns as it does on polylines, including controlling whether the pattern is plotted/printed. One thing, however: if your pattern fill has no boundary, and you turn off fill, your pattern becomes invisible until you turn on fill again.

Managing Many Patterns

The other settings in the **Pattern Settings** dialog box don't change when you pick another pattern. This means that when you set up things like the pattern angle and scale for one pattern, and then select another pattern, the angle and scale remain the same. If you're drawing many different pattern fills, each with different settings, you can lose track of which settings apply to a given pattern. You can do two things to keep track of pattern settings:

- Keep notes of the settings that apply to each pattern fill.

- Use **Show Properties** from the **Measure** menu to find out the settings of an existing pattern fill so that you can draw another the same way or modify the pattern.

Custom Patterns

AutoSketch comes with a lot of patterns (the **.PAT** files in the support directory), but you can add more.

 One way is to get **.PAT** files from someone else: through colleagues (particularly AutoCAD users), commercial sources, and even public domain sources. For the latter, if you're a member of CompuServe (the global online public computer system), look in the Autodesk forum. To get there, type GO ADESK⏎ at any CompuServe prompt.

The other way is to create your own pattern files. It's too complicated to explain in detail (not that it's particularly difficult, just that there are so many commands that make up the script), so look in the appendix in the back of the AutoSketch manual.

Once you have a new pattern file, add it to AutoSketch this way:

1. Store the file in the AutoSketch support directory (by default that's **C:\SKETCH3\SUPPORT**). Simply having this file in that directory adds it to the **Pattern Settings** dialog box, but it won't have an icon. The icon frame will say NO ICON, but you can still click on the name.

2. Follow the procedure in the manual to create an icon, and add it to the file **PATTERN.ICN** in the support directory. After you do that, you'll be able to pick the pattern from its sample picture in the **Pattern Settings** dialog box.

Step 14

Arrays

30

Arrays are regular arrangements of copies of objects. Autodesk has adopted a unique terminology for arrays:

> *Box*   Arrange copies of an object (or objects) in rows
> *arrays*   and columns; the array is rectangular. You con-
> trol the spacing between rows and columns, and
> you can "tilt" the entire array by specifying a
> baseline angle.

> *Ring*   Arrange copies of an object (or objects) in a circle
> *arrays* around a center point. You have control over the
> intricate details: how many copies and how many
> degrees between them, the location of the center
> point, and whether, and how, each copy is rotated
> proportionally to its angle around the circle.

The AutoSketch array commands are true power tools. You could accomplish what they do the hard way (by using the individual **Copy** and **Rotate** commands), but the array commands give you precise control in a single operation.

Box Arrays

It's a straightforward process to create a box array. AutoSketch even lets you specify the row and column distances visually, by dragging an outline of the select object into position. Try it now:

1. Set the snap interval to .25 (and turn on snap, of course), and draw a small box in the lower left corner of the display.

2. Select **Box Array** from the **Change** menu, or press <kbd>Ctrl</kbd>+<kbd>F2</kbd>.

3. `Select object:` Select the box you just drew.

4. `Column spacing First point:` Pick a point below the box.

The exact location isn't important because this is the first of two reference points. The process is just like specifying two points during a copy operation. After you pick this point, AutoSketch displays a highlighted outline of the box, initially located at the same place as the original.

5. To point: Move the pointer to the right, dragging the box outline. When the outline is clear of the original box, click the pointer.

6. Row spacing First point: and To point: Do the same thing to specify the row spacing; pick points to tell AutoSketch the vertical distance between rows.

AutoSketch draws a two-by-two array of copies of the box after you click the second row spacing point. (To be precise, the array consists of three copies and the original.)

7. When AutoSketch displays an **Accept/Modify** dialog box, click **Modify**; let's play with the box array settings.

The **Box Array Settings** dialog box looks like this:

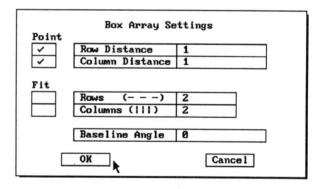

Notice that AutoSketch has recorded the row and column spacing you specified by dragging; this shows you that you can also enter these values into the dialog box if you prefer. The checkmarks in the two Point boxes indicate that spacing is to be specified by pointing, however.

8. Enter **5** into the Rows (– – –) box, and enter **3** into the Columns (| | |) box. In other words, create an array of 5 rows and 3 columns.

9. Enter **45** into the Baseline Angle box; this will tilt the array to the left (counter-clockwise) 45°.

10. Click **OK**. AutoSketch immediately redraws the array with the new settings, and again displays the **Accept/Modify** dialog box. Click **Modify** if you'd like to continue to experiment; otherwise click **Accept**.

One other power feature of the **Box Array** command is controlled by the two checkboxes labeled Fit on the **Box Array Settings** dialog box. The **Fit** checkboxes change the relationship between distance and number of rows or columns, as shown in Table 14.1. As the table shows, in Fit mode, AutoSketch computes the distance between rows or columns (or both) to make the box array fit *within* the specified distance.

Fit off	table width = column distance * number of columns
	distance between columns = column distance
	table height = row distance * number of rows
	distance between rows = row distance
Fit on	table width = column distance
	distance between columns = $\dfrac{\text{column distance}}{\text{number of columns}}$
	table height = row distance
	distance between rows = $\dfrac{\text{row distance}}{\text{number of rows}}$

Table 14.1: The effect of the Fit checkbox on box arrays

Ring Arrays

Ring arrays are a bit more complicated than box arrays because there are several options that let you draw several kinds of ring arrays. Let's start with the default settings:

1. Either clear the display by starting a new file, or pan to an empty area of the drawing space. Draw a small object to work with (a small circle or a box, for example), near the bottom center part of the display.

2. Select **Ring Array** from the **Change** menu, or press Ctrl+F4.

3. Select object: Select the sample object.

4. Center point of array: Pick a point near the center of the display. AutoSketch now draws the ring array using these default settings:

   - Four items in the array.

   - The ring array spans a full 360°, and therefore there is 90° between items.

   - Items are rotated as they are copied.

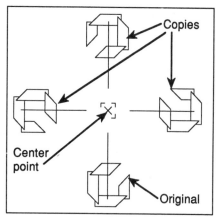

5. AutoSketch displays the **Accept/Modify** dialog box; click **Modify** to experiment. AutoSketch displays the **Ring Array Settings** dialog box, which looks like this:

```
              Ring Array Settings
    Point        Center Point of Array
   ┌─────┐    ┌──────────────────┬──────────┐
   │     │    │ X Coordinate     │ 3        │
   └─────┘    │ Y Coordinate     │ 13       │
             └──────────────────┴──────────┘

             ┌──────────────────┬──────────┐
             │ Number of Items  │ 4        │
             │ Included Angle   │ 360      │
             │ Degrees between Items │ 90  │
             └──────────────────┴──────────┘

             ┌─────┐  Draw Clockwise
             │     │  Rotate Items as Copied
             │  ✓  │  Pivot Point
             └─────┘

        ┌──────────┐           ┌──────────┐
        │   OK     │  ▶        │  Cancel  │
        └──────────┘           └──────────┘
```

The **Center Point of Array** boxes and their associated **Point** checkbox let you control where the center point is. The middle three boxes control how items in the array are arranged.

6. Enter 8 into the **Number of Items** box. Notice that AutoSketch recomputes the **Degrees between Items** to reflect the number, fitting the items into 360°.

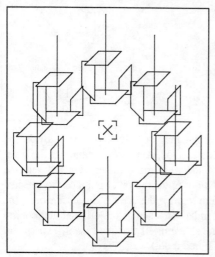

7. Click the **Rotate Items as Copied** checkbox to turn it off.

8. Click **OK**. AutoSketch doesn't immediately redraw the ring array; you must specify the center point again (because **Point** in the dialog box was checked). After you do so, Auto-Sketch redraws the ring array, something like the example to the left.

Notice the effect of turning off **Rotate Items as Copied**. Now the copies have the same orientation as the original.

9.   Click **Modify** in the **Accept/Modify** dialog box.

10. Turn off **Point** (to use the coordinates of the last center point), and click **Pivot Point** to turn it on. Set **Number of Items** to 6. Click **OK**.

11. This time, AutoSketch prompts you for a pivot point. Pick a point to the side of the sample object. AutoSketch again redraws the array, and it looks something like this (minus the circle, which I added to show the relationship of the pivot point to the rotation of the array):

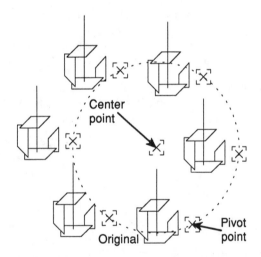

The purpose of the pivot point may be a little obscure. Basically, when you use the pivot point method, AutoSketch translates the pivot point around the circle of the ring array, rather than the selected object(s), and uses the relationship of the pivot point to the selected object(s) to determine where to draw the copies. In other words, the pivot point is a sort of "handle" attached to the original and copies, by which AutoSketch "grabs" them. If that isn't clear, experiment some more (that's how *I* figured it out).

Many of the drawings you'll create with AutoSketch are about physical objects, so you'll want your drawing to communicate information about size and location through *dimensions*. The dimensioning commands on AutoSketch's **Measure** menu insert dimension objects into your drawing; the **Measure** menu also has commands to display information about your drawing, which I'll cover in the next Step.

Here is the terminology I'll use to refer to the parts of a dimension:

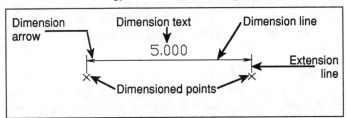

Aligned Dimensions

AutoSketch's simplest dimension type is the *aligned dimension*. Aligned dimension show the distance between any two points, regardless of the angle between them.

1. Use the **Polyline** or **Pattern Fill** command to draw a right triangle.

2. Select **Align Dimension** from the **Measure** menu.

3. `Points to dimension:` Pick one of the vertices adjacent to the hypotenuse.

4. `To point:` Pick the vertex at the other end of the hypotenuse.

5. `Dimension line location:` Pick a point away from the hypotenuse, outside the triangle. This point defines the distance from the object being dimensioned to the dimension line.

AutoSketch draws the dimension line, like this:

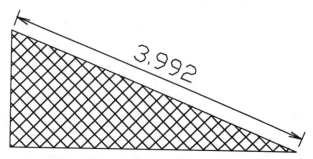

6. Select **Stretch** from the **Change** menu. Select one of the vertices you dimensioned, making sure at least part of the selection box includes the adjacent extension line, and stretch the triangle.

After you select both points, AutoSketch adjusts the dimension text to reflect the new distance. This demonstrates the *associativity* of AutoSketch dimensions—AutoSketch dimensions change to reflect changes in your drawing. Remember, though, that this only works when you include the dimension in any changes.

Horizontal and Vertical Dimensions

These two dimension types are specialized: horizontal dimensions show only the horizontal displacement between two points (ignoring any vertical displacement); and vertical dimensions show only the vertical displacement between two points. Try them out now on your right triangle.

1. Use **Undo** or **Erase** to remove the aligned dimension.

2. Select **Horiz. Dimension** from the **Measure** menu.

3. Pick the two points at each end of the triangle's hypotenuse. Place the dimension line entirely above the triangle by approximately .2 drawing units.

AutoSketch draws the dimension like this:

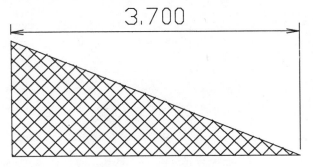

4. Select **Vert. Dimension** from the **Measure** menu.

5. Pick the lower hypotenuse endpoint first, and then the upper endpoint. Place the dimension line outside the triangle.

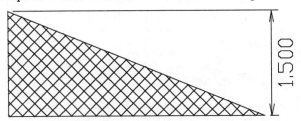

Note that the order in which you pick the points for a vertical dimension is important. If you'd picked the points in the reverse order, AutoSketch would have oriented the dimension text to face the other way.

Angular Dimensions

AutoSketch lets you insert a dimension showing the angle between two lines (or two polyline segments or two edges of a pattern fill). The two lines don't have to intersect, but they can't be parallel. Try it now by dimensioning the angle of your triangle:

1. Select **Angle Dimension** from the **Measure** menu.

2. AutoSketch prompts you to `Select first line` and `Select second line` instead of for dimension points.

Select the two edges of your triangle that form an angle smaller than 90°.

3. `Dimension line arc location:` Pick a point either to the left or right of the triangle.

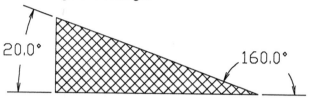

Where you put the dimension line arc–on the interior or exterior of the angle being dimensioned–has a big effect on the result. In the illustration above, the left dimension (20°) is obviously the interior angle. But why doesn't the right dimension show 340° as the angle? It's just a quirk of AutoSketch: it dimensions angles no larger than 180°. If the angle is greater than 180°, AutoSketch subtracts 180° and shows that result. In the illustration, AutoSketch is showing 340°-180°=160°.

Dimension Settings

You can control dimension text (height and font) and the style of arrowhead AutoSketch uses. You already know how to set up text, so let's look at setting the arrow type.

Arrow type is controlled by the **Dimension Arrow Type** dialog box, which is displayed when you select **Arrow** from the **Settings** menu. The dialog box and the arrow types look like this:

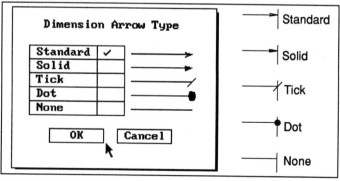

Step 16

Measuring Objects

In this Step you'll learn about the second group of commands on the **Measure** menu: the commands that display information about objects in a drawing. These commands are passive—they display information about objects and don't modify your drawing in any way.

Except for **Show Properties** (which reads the drawing database to display information about an object), the commands don't have to measure existing objects. Rather, they display information (such as distance or angle) about points you pick. Of course, these commands are most useful when the points correspond to real objects. You'll generally want to use one of the attach modes to tie your picks to objects.

Displaying Distance and Location

The **Distance** command shows you the distance between two points. Try it now:

Showing distance

1. Select **Distance** from the **Measure** menu.

2. In response to the two prompts, pick two points (for this exercise, the exact locations don't matter).

    AutoSketch displays a message box showing the distance in drawing units between the two points.

3. When you've read the information, click **OK**.

Easy, wasn't it? All the rest of the information commands work the same way. The **Point** command shows location, and it's so simple, it almost doesn't need instructions:

Showing location

1. Turn on the coordinate display.

2. Select **Point** from the **Measure** menu.

3. Click the pointer somewhere.

AutoSketch displays a message box showing the coordinates of the location where you clicked. These coordinates should match the location shown in the coordinate display.

4. Click **OK** to remove the message box.

Displaying Bearing and Angle

Bearing

These two commands deal with angles. The **Bearing** command shows the direction from one point to a second point, like this:

1. Select **Bearing** from the **Measure** menu.

2. Pick a point.

3. Move the pointer away from the first point, at approximately a 45° angle, and then click the pointer.

    AutoSketch displays a message box showing the exact bearing of the second point from the first.

4. Click **OK** to put away the message box.

Showing the angle between two lines

The **Angle** command also deals with angles. In its case, the **Angle** command measures the angle formed by two imaginary lines connecting three points (the two lines have one common point). In this exercise you'll use an attach mode to learn how to measure existing objects.

1. Select the endpoint-attachment method, and turn on attach mode.

2. Draw a line that's roughly horizontal. Then draw a second line starting at the left endpoint of the first line (that's the common point between the lines). Draw the second line up and to the right of the first line.

3. Select **Angle** from the **Measure** menu.

4. `Base point:` Pick the point that's common to both lines.

5. `First direction:` Pick the opposite end of the first line.

6. Second direction: Pick the end of the second line.

   AutoSketch displays a message box showing the angle formed by the two lines.

7. Click **OK** when you've read the information.

Displaying Area

AutoSketch's **Area** command measures the area contained within a perimeter that you specify. This perimeter is made up of straight line segments only (connecting the points you pick). Thus, if you're measuring a curved area, you can only approximate the area within the curve. In this situation you should pick as many perimeter points as you have patience for, to make the result as accurate as possible. Try it out:

1. Draw a closed polyline or pattern fill with at least five vertices (four would make a rectangle, and would be no challenge at all).

2. Select **Area** from the **Measure** menu.

3. First perimeter point: Pick one of the vertices of the polyline or pattern fill (endpoint-attach should still be on, simplifying this task). AutoSketch displays an X at this point to remind you where you began.

4. Next point: Pick the rest of the vertices, in sequence one direction or the other, around the polyline or pattern fill. AutoSketch marks each point with an X that's smaller than the first, to let you keep track of your progress.

5. After you've picked all the vertices, you should be back at the first point. Click this point again to finish the perimeter. Notice that this is just like drawing a polyline or pattern fill border.

   AutoSketch displays a message box showing the area, in drawing units, contained within the perimeter. This box also shows the length of the perimeter.

6. Click **OK** to put away the message box.

Displaying Properties

The **Show properties** command displays the properties of an object you select. When you pick an object, AutoSketch reads the drawing database and displays the information from the database. It's quite simple; try it on one of the lines you drew earlier to test it.

I've found **Show properties** most useful with text. When you're creating a drawing with several styles of text, it's easy to lose track of the font name, size, or other parameters for various text objects. After using **Show properties** on an existing piece of text, you can change the text settings to match the properties and draw more text with the same settings. Almost as often, I've used this command to find out which layer an object is on; this saves me from having to turn layers off until the object I'm interested in disappears. In general, **Show properties** is most useful in situations where the property you're interested in might not be visible, or you can't accurately judge the property just by looking at it (two examples are polyline width, and pattern fill scale and angle).

Parts are AutoSketch drawings you insert into your current drawing. You can set up libraries of drawing files containing symbols you use in your work: plumbing and electrical fixture symbols if you're an architect, electronic symbols if you're an engineer, and so on. You can use existing drawings as parts, or you can create part (drawing) files by copying selected objects from your current file into another file.

When you insert a part, AutoSketch shows an outline of the part, and that outline moves with the pointer. The outline is attached to the pointer by its *part base*. The part base of a drawing is 0,0 by default; you can set it to some other more meaningful location (like the center or one corner of the part) if you want to.

For this exercise, let's set up the BALL and ROD drawings you created earlier as parts, and then insert them into a new drawing. Along the way, you'll learn about the three ways you can control the part base of a part drawing.

Using the Default Part Base

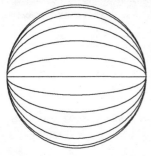

The default part base is 0,0. Use the default if 0,0 is meaningful for the part. We'll start with the BALL drawing, and make 0,0 correspond to the center of the ball.

1. Open the **BALL** drawing from Step 7.

2. Erase the "scaffolding"–every-thing except the ball.

3. Use the **Redraw** command to clean up the display.

4. You'll see that erasing the scaffolding also left the ball without a horizontal center line. Turn on endpoint-attach mode and add the line across the center of the ball.

5. Group the ball (use a crosses selection box to make sure you get everything, including the center line).

6. Set attach mode to center-attach and set all other attachment methods off. Turn on attach.

7. Select **Move** from the **Change** menu.

8. Pick the grouped ball.

9. From point: Pick one of the ellipses in the ball; center-attach mode selects the center of the ball.

10. To point: Type 0,0 ⏎.

    AutoSketch moves the ball so that its center is at 0,0. This probably means that the ball disappears after it's moved.

11. Use **Zoom Full** to display the ball in its new location.

12. Save the **BALL** drawing.

Copying Objects to a Part File

You can copy objects from your current drawing to another file; you do this with the **Part Clip** command. Use it now to create a part file containing the tilted rod.

1. Open the **ROD** drawing. If you completed the exercises in Step 9, it should contain two rods, one of them tilted.

2. Group each rod (individually).

3. Turn on center-attach mode (you have to do this again because this is a different drawing, and its stored settings will be different).

4. Select **Part Clip** from the **File** menu.

5. AutoSketch displays a dialog box asking for a name for this part file. Enter **ROD-TILT** and click **OK**.

6. Part insertion base: Pick the left edge of the ellipse at the left side of the tilted rod. Center-attach mode selects the center of the ellipse as the part base.

7. Select object: Pick the tilted rod. After you pick the tilted rod, AutoSketch highlights it.

8. Select **Erase** from the **Change** menu. Notice that picking another command terminates **Part Clip**, in the same manner as the **Group** command.

9. Erase the tilted rod (it now exists in its own file).

Setting the Part Base Manually

You can specify a part base other than the default 0,0 with the **Part Base** command on the **Settings** menu. Use it now to make the center of the left ellipse of the remaining rod this drawing's base point.

1. Select **Part Base** from the **Settings** menu.

2. In the **Part Insertion Base Point** dialog box, click **Default Base Point**; this tells AutoSketch that you want to set the file's base point using the pointer. Click **OK**.

   Leaving the other checkbox—**Part Clip Base Point**—checked doesn't have any effect on this operation.

3. Pick the left edge of the left ellipse. Center-attach selects the center of the ellipse as the drawing's base point.

4. Select **New** from the **File** menu; when AutoSketch displays the **Save/Discard/Cancel** dialog box, click **Save**.

Inserting Parts into a Drawing

You now have three parts: a ball, a horizontal rod, and a tilted rod. It's time to use them to create a drawing.

1. Select **Part** from the **Draw** menu.

2. AutoSketch displays a file selection dialog box. Select **BALL** and click **OK**.

AutoSketch loads the BALL drawing and displays an outline of the ball attached to the pointer at the ball's center.

3. Move the pointer so that the ball outline is in the lower left corner of the display, and click. AutoSketch draws the ball at this location.

4. Repeat steps 1 and 2 above, this time inserting **ROD**. Position the rod so that it's "attached" to the ball (see the example below).

5. Insert **ROD-TILT** this time. The result should look like this:

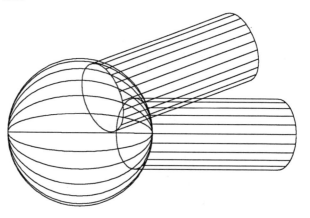

6. Save the drawing if you plan to experiment further.

That's all there is to AutoSketch's part facility. As an optional exercise (if you're feeling ambitious), recreate the cube optical illusion from Step 7; you now have all the parts, as well as the skills, you need. The biggest challenge is breaking the lines and ellipses in the balls and rods so that they appear to merge. Some hints: you'll have to ungroup each part to use the **Break** command on its component objects, and you'll have to use intersection-attach mode to break objects where they meet other objects.

Plotting and Printing

You must have thought we'd never get around to plotting or printing your drawings. Well, the moment has arrived! In this Step you'll learn how to plot or print.

I'll assume you've configured AutoSketch to use an output device. Since AutoSketch can use either plotters or printers, for simplicity I'll just call the process *plotting*. AutoSketch changes the wording of several **File** menu commands from "Plot" to "Print," depending on whether you've configured AutoSketch to use a plotter or a printer.

Simple Plotting

Plotting has been improved in AutoSketch Version 3 to the point where most of the things you had to set up in earlier versions are now done automatically for you. This means that you can just go ahead and plot, and AutoSketch will scale your drawing automatically to fill up the page as completely as possible. Give it a try:

1. Load one of the drawings you created earlier, or open a sample drawing.

2. Select **Plot** from the **File** menu (the command will be **Print** if you configured AutoSketch to use a printer).

While AutoSketch is plotting, it displays Plotting... in the prompt line. After a while (depending on the complexity of the drawing), your drawing should emerge from the plotter or printer.

Plot Boxes

A *plot box* is a rectangle that defines the area of your drawing to be plotted. The plot box itself doesn't plot but is displayed on the screen along with its dimensions. The size of the plot box is usually equal to the plottable area of the paper selected for your plotter or printer (although you can specify another plot box size, as long as it will fit on to the selected paper). The ratio of the plot box size to the size of your drawing determines the scale of what's plotted.

Let's try it first by fitting the plot box snugly around a drawing (you should still have a drawing loaded).

1. Select **Plot Area** (or **Print Area**) from the **File** menu. AutoSketch displays the **Paper Size** dialog box:

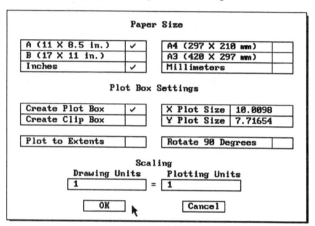

Notice that the top several boxes in this dialog box let you set the paper size; the paper sizes listed depend on the plotter or printer you've configured AutoSketch to use. I'll discuss the other boxes a bit later.

2. Turn on **Plot to Extents**; this tells AutoSketch to make the plot box just fit around your drawing's extents. Notice that the number in the **Drawing Units** box will change as AutoSketch computes the scale for the drawing.

3. Click **OK**. AutoSketch redraws the screen showing the plot box around the contents of the drawing; then AutoSketch displays an **Accept/Modify** dialog box.

4. Click **Accept**. (If you click **Modify**, you'll return to the **Paper Size** dialog box.).

5. Select **Last Plot Box** from the **View** menu to redraw the display so that the plot box fills up your display.

6. Select **Plot** (or **Print**) from the **File** menu.

Advanced Plot Boxes

The **Paper Size** dialog box has several more options that let you precisely control how your drawing is plotted.

The scale at which your drawing is plotted is controlled by the ratio between the values in the **Drawing Units** and **Plotting Units** boxes. Usually you'll enter a new value into one of the boxes and leave the other set to 1; but you don't have to. You can use these two boxes to set up a ratio, for example, for unit conversions. You must turn off **Plot to Extents** to manually scale the plot box.

Scaling the plot

X Plot Size and **Y Plot Size** set the size of the plot box. By default they're set to the maximum printable area of your output device. You can make these values smaller, but not larger. When I created the drawings for this book, I set the plot box width to equal the width of the drawings as they appear here, and then used **Plot to Extents** so that I didn't have to rescale the drawings later.

Plot box size

If you create a plot box that's smaller than the drawing extents, only the part of the drawing within the plot box plots. You can use **Move** to move the plot box around to plot different areas of the drawing; this might be useful if you want to splice together several sheets to make a larger plot. You can also use **Scale** to make the plot box larger or smaller.

Changing a plot box

You can erase a plot box, and then use **Plot Area** (or **Print Area**) to create a new one. You can have several plot boxes in a drawing at once, but only one can be visible when you plot; if more than one is visible, AutoSketch displays an error message. The way to manage multiple plot boxes is to put them on several different layers, and then turn on only the layer with the plot box you want to use.

Managing multiple plot boxes

The **Rotate 90 Degrees** checkbox controls the orientation of your drawing on the paper. Turning it on swaps the values in the **X Plot Size** and **Y Plot Size** boxes. If you're using a printer, this means that the printout will be in portrait orientation by default (**Rotate 90 Degrees** off) and in landscape orientation when you turn on this checkbox.

Plot orientation

Clip Boxes

The **Create Plot Box** checkbox controls whether AutoSketch creates a plot box. It's possible to do this because you can also use the **Paper Size** dialog box to create a *clip box*, either with or without a plot box. A clip box defines a region, within a plot box, that will be plotted; any of the drawing outside the clip box—even if it's within the plot box—won't be printed.

The clip box starts out about three-quarters of the size of the plot box. You can move it and scale it to fit the area you want to print, and you can stretch a clip box to change its shape. You can also move it to a different layer to control whether you use it with a given plot.

Plotting/Printing to a File

When you configure AutoSketch, you're asked which port connects your computer to the output device. One of the choices is "File," which means that AutoSketch stores output commands in a file instead of sending them to the plotter or printer. This can be useful if you want to save long plot jobs for printing later (such as at night, after you go home for the day). It's also one way you can exchange AutoSketch drawings with other programs; I'll cover this subject in detail in the next Step.

If you've configured AutoSketch to plot to a file, the **Plot Name** (or **Print Name**) command on the **File** menu is activated. It displays a dialog box for you to enter the name of an output file. Enter just the name; all output files are given the extension **.PLT**.

Pen Information

If you're using a plotter, the **Pen Info** command on the **File** menu lets you assign "entity colors" (the colors of objects in your drawing) to pen numbers. You can also set the pen speed in case your plotter's pens skip at the highest speed settings.

Step 19

Exchanging Drawings

Most people use AutoSketch all by itself to produce drawings only in AutoSketch that are only plotted or printed; they never have to worry about transferring their work to other programs. However, don't overlook the possibility of exchanging AutoSketch drawings with other programs. This opens up a world of possibilities, from embedding drawings in engineering reports and technical manuals, to "touching up" AutoSketch drawings in another drawing program.

As shown in Figure 19.1 below, AutoSketch has several interfaces that let you transform a drawing file into some other file format. This handful of interfaces is sufficient to let you exchange a drawing with just about any other program—one way or another. Sometimes getting from AutoSketch to another program requires you to take a twisted path through conversion programs and the other program's import or export commands. Somehow, though, there's a way to get the job done. There are too many ways to exchange drawings to cover them all here, so I'll just describe the interfaces, and then use my own experience writing this book as one case study. You might get some ideas from my experiences that you can extrapolate into your own situation.

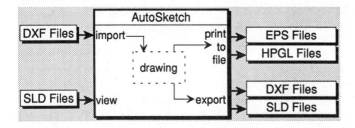

Figure 19.1: AutoSketch's import and export interfaces

DXF Files

DXF stands for *Drawing Interchange Format*. It was developed originally by Autodesk as the interchange format used by Auto-CAD and was included in AutoSketch so that you can easily move your drawings up to AutoCAD. DXF has been widely adopted by many software vendors and has become a defacto standard for exchanging files.

Of all the ways you can import or export drawings with Auto-Sketch, DXF preserves the most information about a drawing. You can export your drawing to a DXF file and then read it back in, and it will contain all the features of the original. So, use DXF if the other program supports it.

Exporting a DXF file

To export your drawing in DXF format, select **Make DXF** from the **File** menu. When asked, give the file a name; don't include the extension since AutoSketch adds the extension **.DXF** automatically.

Importing a DXF file

To import a DXF file, select **Read DXF** from the **File** menu. Select the file from the file selection box.

Caveats

While you can count on an Autodesk product to implement DXF correctly, several other vendors have had problems with it. Part of the reason is that DXF is being continually extended as Autodesk products grow in complexity, and the other vendors have to scramble to update their own DXF implementations. You'll have to test it and see if it works. I've tried it with Micrografx Designer 3.01 and couldn't get several of my DXF files to import accurately at all.

Another thing to be aware of is that the receiving program usually requires access to the font shape files used to create the drawing. If the receiving program is on the same computer on which you're running AutoSketch, that's usually no problem. If the receiving program is on another computer, resist the temptation to also provide that other computer with a copy of the shape files; that would violate the license agreement you agreed to when you opened the shrink-wrapped package. Instead, the other computer should have its own licensed copy of AutoSketch, or you should arrange to perform the conversion on your own computer.

Encapsulated PostScript

You can have AutoSketch export a drawing in Encapsulated PostScript (EPS) format if you're using a PostScript printer or typesetting machine. AutoSketch's EPS files include all the standard EPS PostScript commands, but they don't include a TIFF preview image (don't worry if that doesn't mean anything to you—most programs will sort out the difference automatically).

To create EPS files, configure AutoSketch to use a PostScript printer, and tell AutoSketch to print to a file. The files will have the extension **.PLT**; you can rename them in DOS to use the more standard **.EPS** extension. Don't check **Rotate 90 degrees** in the **Paper Size** dialog box unless you really want the image to appear sideways when it's later printed; most desktop publishing and word processing programs can't rotate an imported EPS image for you.

Creating an EPS file

EPS files are "read only"; that is, the program receiving them can't modify them and can only print them. In general, the receiving program will have an import command that lists EPS as one of its options; refer to your program's documentation for more information. I've used AutoSketch EPS files with Microsoft Word 5.0 (with no problems) and Word for Windows (with some problems due to the EPS macro supplied by Microsoft).

HPGL Files

HPGL stands for *Hewlett-Packard Graphics Language*, and it's the command language used by all HP plotters. Many graphics and word processing programs support it as well. Unlike EPS, HPGL is printer-independent. That's because HPGL is really just a list of the motions a pen would make as it plots the drawing, and all the receiving or conversion program has to do is map those pen strokes to another format. The drawback is that the file records no information about the objects that made up the original drawing—curves become sequences of short straight lines, solid polylines are filled with many short line strokes, and so on. Thus, if you use HPGL to import your drawing into another graphics program, you'll end up with a very large number of small lines, which you'll probably have to edit to simplify into objects.

Creating
an HPGL
file

Configure AutoSketch to use an HP model 7550 plotter and to plot to a file. Then use the **Plot Area, Plot Name,** and **Plot** commands as described in the last Step. You may want to rename the files in DOS to use the common **.PGL** extension. Again, don't check **Rotate 90 degrees** unless you really want the image to be plotted sideways.

I've found that I get the best results by selecting the largest paper size available in the **Paper Size** dialog box and plotting to extents. This forces the plotter driver to "draw" the plot as large as possible, using the largest number of short pen strokes, and thus give the highest resolution in the output.

Word-
Perfect

If you want to use an AutoSketch drawing in a WordPerfect drawing, use WordPerfect's GRAPHCNV utility to convert the HPGL format file to WordPerfect's own WPG format.

Microsoft
Word

Microsoft Word 5.0 and later (for DOS) can use HPGL files. Use the **Library/Link/Graphics** command, and tell Word that it's an HPGL file.

SLD Files

SLD files are "slide" files. They're a bit of an enigma, being "neither fish nor fowl." They're a snapshot of the AutoSketch display at the time they're created, but the data is stored as a sequence of "strokes" rather than a simple bitmap image (like an ordinary screen capture). Because they're a screen image, SLD files can have no more resolution (another way of saying "quality") than your display can provide.

SLD files are not used much in desktop publishing because of their poor resolution. Ventura Publisher can read them, but since Ventura also reads DXF files, it's a mystery to me why anyone would use SLD files. Still, they may be your last resort if Ventura can't read a particular DXF file.

To create a slide file, use the **View** menu commands to frame the view of your drawing you want made into a slide. Then select the **Make Slide** command from the **File** menu. Give the file a name when asked.

AutoSketch can also view slide files; use **View Slide** on the **View** menu. The slide file temporarily replaces the view of your drawing on the display, but it doesn't become part of the drawing. Any command that redraws the display clears the slide image from the display.

How I Produced This Book

At the beginning of this Step, I commented that you sometimes have to take a twisted path to import AutoSketch drawings into another program. Now you'll see what I meant.

First of all, I'm using Microsoft Windows 3.0. It turns out that you can run AutoSketch under Windows 3.0; you run it full-screen as a regular DOS application. The Windows installation program even found the AutoSketch program files and correctly created an icon in Program Manager.

However: **running AutoSketch under Windows 3.0 is not officially supported by Autodesk.** If it works for you, great; if not, you're on your own. Remember, also, that AutoSketch isn't a Windows application: there are no Windows "hooks" like copy and paste to the clipboard.

Running AutoSketch under Windows means that you can switch back and forth between AutoSketch and other programs. This allowed me to create drawings in AutoSketch, export them, import them in Microsoft Word for Windows, and go back to AutoSketch to make changes if I didn't like the result. However, that's quite an oversimplification—here's the twisted path I had to take:

1. I configured AutoSketch to use an HP plotter and print to a file; in other words, I worked with HPGL files.

2. I plotted each drawing to a file and changed its extension from **.PLT** to **.PGL**.

3. Then I used a graphics conversion program called Hijaak 2.0 to convert the files from HPGL format to CGM (Computer Graphics Metafile) format.

   I chose CGM because Micrografx Designer could import CGM (and also because of the problems with Designer's DXF import that I noted earlier). The combination of HPGL and CGM meant that the drawings as printed in the book would closely resemble how the drawings would look plotted or printed. This was most useful when I wanted to show AutoSketch text because HPGL recorded the appearance of the text as the sequence of pen strokes required to draw it, and thus gave me the most realistic results.

4. In Micrografx Designer 3.0 I imported the CGM files. Often, I added callouts and arrows to annotate the drawing.

   This is an example of how you can use another program to touch up an AutoSketch drawing. I erased the lines making up the original CAD text and substituted "real" text. That's how the AutoSketch drawings in this book ended up using nice printer fonts, even though I told you in Step 6 that you couldn't do that.

5. After selecting the drawing, I copied it to the Windows clipboard.

6. In Word for Windows, with one of the book files open, I pasted the image into the proper location.

Yes, that was a very convoluted way to import AutoSketch drawings into Word for Windows. But it worked. The important lesson from this example is not that you have to duplicate how I did it; rather, if you apply the general principles you'll always—somehow—succeed in importing AutoSketch drawings into another program. The most important point is this: even if two programs don't share a common file format, you can pass the drawings through a conversion program, or even another application, and eventually end up with a file format your program can read.

Macros

AutoSketch has a rudimentary macro facility that records where you click the pointer and what you type, and later plays back the record. I have to call it "rudimentary" so that you don't expect to be able to program AutoSketch; I want to set your expectations for AutoSketch macros appropriately low. AutoSketch can only record and play back your actions; while you can perform some minor editing on the record file, you can't really program Auto-Sketch in any meaningful sense. However, since AutoSketch's macro facility can come in handy, let's explore how to use it.

Recording and Playing Back a Macro

In this exercise you'll record a macro that draws a star. You'll tell AutoSketch to wait for you to enter the first coordinates when the macro is played back. The rest of the macro will use relative coordinates so that you can use the macro to draw a star at different locations when you play it back.

1. Select **Record Macro** from the **Assist** menu.

2. Select **Polyline** from the **Draw** menu.

3. First point: Press Ctrl+F10 to tell AutoSketch to pause at this point when it plays back the macro and to not record what you type now (while you're creating the macro); this allows you to enter something different when you play back the macro. Then enter 4,1⏎ as the first point of the polyline.

4. Enter the remaining points for this polyline:

   r(3,7)⏎
   r(3,-7)⏎
   r(-6,4)⏎
   r(6,0)⏎
   r(-6,-4) ⏎ (the last point completes the polyline)

5. Select **End Macro** from the **Assist** menu (it's in the same position as **Record Macro**; AutoSketch changes the name when you start recording). AutoSketch is no longer recording.

6. Select **Play Macro** from the **Assist** menu.

    AutoSketch doesn't seem to do anything. That's because the second action you recorded, after selecting **Polyline**, was the `Ctrl`+`F10` command to pause. The result: AutoSketch waits for you to pick the first point of the star.

7. Click with the pointer or type coordinates to set the first point of the polyline star.

    Either clicking the pointer or pressing `⏎` ends the pause and lets AutoSketch proceed, which it does now, drawing the rest of the star.

If you make a mistake while you're recording, you have no choice but to select **End Macro** and then **Record Macro** to start over. You can't back up over recorded actions. It's possible to edit the macro record file, which is just an ASCII file, but that's more trouble than it's worth unless you're recording a very long macro. If you want to edit a macro file, see the appendix on the macro language in the AutoSketch manual.

You can also record the actions you take while working in dialog boxes. This might be useful if you want to record a standard group of settings you use in all drawings; this saves you the time you'd otherwise spend manually setting them.

Macro Files

The macro you just recorded is stored automatically in a file called **SKETCH.MCR**. If you record a new macro, the old record in the file is overwritten and lost. To permanently save a macro file, give it a new name by selecting **Make Macro** from the **File** menu. Later, you can play back that file, instead of the default **SKETCH.MCR**, by selecting **Read Macro**.

Index

Selections from The SYBEX Library

CAD

The ABC's of AutoCAD
(Second Edition)
Alan R. Miller
375pp. Ref. 584-0
This brief but effective introduction to AutoCAD quickly gets users drafting and designing with this complex CADD package. The essential operations and capabilities of AutoCAD are neatly detailed, using a proven, step-by-step method that is tailored to the results-oriented beginner.

The ABC's of AutoLISP
George Omura
300pp. Ref. 620-0
This book is for users who want to unleash the full power of AutoCAD through the AutoLISP programming language. In non-technical terms, the reader is shown how to store point locations, create new commands, and manipulate coordinates and text. Packed with tips on common coding errors.

The ABC's of Generic CADD
Alan R. Miller
278pp. Ref. 608-1
This outstanding guide to computer-aided design and drafting with Generic CADD assumes no previous experience with computers or CADD. This book will have users doing useful CADD work in record time, including basic drawing with the keyboard or a mouse, erasing and unerasing, making a copy of drawings on your printer, adding text and organizing your drawings using layers.

Advanced Techniques in AutoCAD (Second Edition)
Robert M. Thomas
425pp. Ref. 593-X
Develop custom applications using screen menus, command macros, and AutoLISP programming—no prior programming experience required. Topics include customizing the AutoCAD environment, advanced data extraction techniques, and much more.

AutoCAD Desktop Companion
SYBEX Ready Reference Series
Robert M. Thomas
1094pp. Ref. 590-5
This is a complete reference work covering all the features, commands, and user options available under AutoCAD Release 10, including drawing basic and complex entities, editing, displaying, printing, plotting, and customizing drawings, manipulating the drawing database, and AutoLISP programming. Through Release 10.

AutoCAD Instant Reference
SYBEX Prompter Series
George Omura
390pp. Ref. 548-4, 4 ¾" × 8"
This pocket-sized reference is a quick guide to all AutoCAD features. Designed for easy use, all commands are organized with exact syntax, a brief description, options, tips, and references. Through Release 10.

Mastering AutoCAD Release 11
George Omura
1150pp, Ref. 716-9
Even if you're just beginning, this comprehensive guide will help you to become an AutoCAD expert. Create your first drawing, then learn to use dimensions, enter pre-existing drawings, use advanced 3-D features, and more. Suitable for experienced users, too—includes tips and tricks you won't find elsewhere.

Mastering VersaCAD
David Bassett-Parkins
450pp. Ref. 617-0
For every level of VCAD user, this comprehensive tutorial treats each phase of

project design including drawing, modifying, grouping, and filing. The reader will also learn VCAD project management and many tips, tricks, and shortcuts. Version 5.4.

OPERATING SYSTEMS

The ABC's of DOS 4
Alan R. Miller
275pp. Ref. 583-2
This step-by-step introduction to using DOS 4 is written especially for beginners. Filled with simple examples, *The ABC's of DOS 4* covers the basics of hardware, software, disks, the system editor EDLIN, DOS commands, and more.

ABC's of MS-DOS
(Second Edition)
Alan R. Miller
233pp. Ref. 493-3
This handy guide to MS-DOS is all many PC users need to manage their computer files, organize floppy and hard disks, use EDLIN, and keep their computers organized. Additional information is given about utilities like Sidekick, and there is a DOS command and program summary. The second edition is fully updated for Version 3.3.

DOS Assembly Language Programming
Alan R. Miller
365pp. 487-9
This book covers PC-DOS through 3.3, and gives clear explanations of how to assemble, link, and debug 8086, 8088, 80286, and 80386 programs. The example assembly language routines are valuable for students and programmers alike.

DOS Instant Reference
SYBEX Prompter Series
Greg Harvey
Kay Yarborough Nelson
220pp. Ref. 477-1, 4 ¾" × 8"
A complete fingertip reference for fast, easy on-line help:command summaries, syntax, usage and error messages. Organized by function—system commands, file commands, disk management, directories,

batch files, I/O, networking, programming, and more. Through Version 3.3.

Encyclopedia DOS
Judd Robbins
1030pp. Ref. 699-5
A comprehensive reference and user's guide to all versions of DOS through 4.0. Offers complete information on every DOS command, with all possible switches and parameters—plus examples of effective usage. An invaluable tool.

Essential OS/2
(Second Edition)
Judd Robbins
445pp. Ref. 609-X
Written by an OS/2 expert, this is the guide to the powerful new resources of the OS/2 operating system standard edition 1.1 with presentation manager. Robbins introduces the standard edition, and details multitasking under OS/2, and the range of commands for installing, starting up, configuring, and running applications. For Version 1.1 Standard Edition.

Essential PC-DOS
(Second Edition)
Myril Clement Shaw
Susan Soltis Shaw
332pp. Ref. 413-5
An authoritative guide to PC-DOS, including version 3.2. Designed to make experts out of beginners, it explores everything from disk management to batch file programming. Includes an 85-page command summary. Through Version 3.2.

Graphics Programming Under Windows
Brian Myers
Chris Doner
646pp. Ref. 448-8
Straightforward discussion, abundant examples, and a concise reference guide to graphics commands make this book a must for Windows programmers. Topics range from how Windows works to programming for business, animation, CAD, and desktop publishing. For Version 2.

Hard Disk Instant Reference
SYBEX Prompter Series
Judd Robbins
256pp. Ref. 587-5, 4 ¾" × 8"
Compact yet comprehensive, this pocket-sized reference presents the essential information on DOS commands used in

managing directories and files, and in optimizing disk configuration. Includes a survey of third-party utility capabilities. Through DOS 4.0.

Inside DOS: A Programmer's Guide
Michael J. Young
490pp. Ref. 710-X
A collection of practical techniques (with source code listings) designed to help you take advantage of the rich resources intrinsic to MS-DOS machines. Designed for the experienced programmer with a basic understanding of C and 8086 assembly language, and DOS fundamentals.

Mastering DOS (Second Edition)
Judd Robbins
722pp. Ref. 555-7
"The most useful DOS book." This seven-part, in-depth tutorial addresses the needs of users at all levels. Topics range from running applications, to managing files and directories, configuring the system, batch file programming, and techniques for system developers. Through Version 4.

MS-DOS Power User's Guide, Volume I (Second Edition)
Jonathan Kamin
482pp. Ref. 473-9
A fully revised, expanded edition of our best-selling guide to high-performance DOS techniques and utilities—with details on Version 3.3. Configuration, I/O, directory structures, hard disks, RAM disks, batch file programming, the ANSI.SYS device driver, more. Through Version 3.3.

Understanding DOS 3.3
Judd Robbins
678pp. Ref. 648-0
This best selling, in-depth tutorial addresses the needs of users at all levels with many examples and hands-on exercises. Robbins discusses the fundamentals of DOS, then covers manipulating files and directories, using the DOS editor, printing, communicating, and finishes with a full section on batch files.

Understanding Hard Disk Management on the PC
Jonathan Kamin
500pp. Ref. 561-1
This title is a key productivity tool for all hard disk users who want efficient, error-free file management and organization. Includes details on the best ways to conserve hard disk space when using several memory-guzzling programs. Through DOS 4.

Up & Running with Your Hard Disk
Klaus M Rubsam
140pp. Ref. 666-9
A far-sighted, compact introduction to hard disk installation and basic DOS use. Perfect for PC users who want the practical essentials in the shortest possible time. In 20 basic steps, learn to choose your hard disk, work with accessories, back up data, use DOS utilities to save time, and more.

Up & Running with Windows 286/386
Gabriele Wentges
132pp. Ref. 691-X
This handy 20-step overview gives PC users all the essentials of using Windows—whether for evaluating the software, or getting a fast start. Each self-contained lesson takes just 15 minutes to one hour to complete.

DESKTOP PUBLISHING

The ABC's of the New Print Shop
Vivian Dubrovin
340pp. Ref. 640-4
This beginner's guide stresses fun, practicality and original ideas. Hands-on tutorials show how to create greeting cards, invitations, signs, flyers, letterheads, banners, and calendars.

The ABC's of Ventura
Robert Cowart
Steve Cummings
390pp. Ref. 537-9
Created especially for new desktop publishers, this is an easy introduction to a complex program. Cowart provides details on using the mouse, the Ventura side bar, and page layout, with careful explanations of publishing terminology. The new Ventura menus are all carefully explained. For Version 2.

Mastering CorelDRAW!
Steve Rimmer
403pp. Ref. 685-5
This four-color tutorial and user's guide covers drawing and tracing, text and special effects, file interchange, and adding new fonts. With in-depth treatment of design principles. For version 1.1.

Mastering PageMaker on the IBM PC (Second Edition)
Antonia Stacy Jolles
384pp. Ref. 521-2
A guide to every aspect of desktop publishing with PageMaker: the vocabulary and basics of page design, layout, graphics and typography, plus instructions for creating finished typeset publications of all kinds.

Mastering Ventura for Windows (For Version 3.0)
Rick Altman
600pp, Ref. 758-4
This engaging, hands-on treatment is for the desktop publisher learning and using the Windows edition of Ventura. It covers everything from working with the Windows interface, to designing and printing sophisticated publications using Ventura's most advanced features. Understand and work with frames, graphics, fonts, tables and columns, and much more.

Mastering Ventura 3.0 Gem Edition
Matthew Holtz
650pp, Ref. 703-7
The complete hands-on guide to desktop publishing with Xerox Ventura Publisher—now in an up-to-date new edition featuring Ventura version 3.0, with the GEM windowing environment. Tutorials cover every aspect of the software, with examples ranging from correspondence and press releases, to newsletters, technical documents, and more.

Understanding PFS: First Publisher
Gerry Litton
310pp. Ref. 616-2
This complete guide takes users from the basics all the way through the most complex features available. Discusses working with text and graphics, columns, clip art, and add-on software enhancements. Many page layout suggestions are introduced. Includes Fast Track speed notes.

Understanding PostScript Programming (Second Edition)
David A. Holzgang
472pp. Ref. 566-2
In-depth treatment of PostScript for programmers and advanced users working on custom desktop publishing tasks. Hands-on development of programs for font creation, integrating graphics, printer implementations and more.

Ventura Instant Reference SYBEX Prompter Series
Matthew Holtz
320pp. Ref. 544-1, 4 ¾" × 8"
This compact volume offers easy access to the complex details of Ventura modes and options, commands, side-bars, file management, output device configuration, and control. Written for versions through Ventura 2, it also includes standard procedures for project and job control.

Ventura Power Tools
Rick Altman
318pp. Ref. 592-1
Renowned Ventura expert, Rick Altman, presents strategies and techniques for the most efficient use of Ventura Publisher 2. This includes a power disk with DOS utilities which is specially designed for optimizing Ventura use. Learn how to soup up Ventura, edit CHP files, avoid design tragedies, handle very large documents, and improve form.

Your HP LaserJet Handbook
Alan R. Neibauer
564pp. Ref. 618-9
Get the most from your printer with this step-by-step instruction book for using

LaserJet text and graphics features such as cartridge and soft fonts, type selection, memory and processor enhancements, PCL programming, and PostScript solutions. This hands-on guide provides specific instructions for working with a variety of software.

NETWORKS

The ABC's of Local Area Networks
Michael Dortch
212pp. Ref. 664-2
This jargon-free introduction to LANs is for current and prospective users who see general information, comparative options, a look at the future, and tips for effective LANs use today. With comparisons of Token-Ring, PC Network, Novell, and others.

The ABC's of Novell Netware
Jeff Woodward
282pp. Ref. 614-6
For users who are new to PC's or networks, this entry-level tutorial outlines each basic element and operation of Novell. The ABC's introduces computer hardware and software, DOS, network organization and security, and printing and communicating over the netware system.

Mastering Novell Netware
Cheryl C. Currid
Craig A. Gillett
500pp. Ref. 630-8
This book is a thorough guide for System Administrators to installing and operating a microcomputer network using Novell Netware. Mastering covers actually setting up a network from start to finish, design, administration, maintenance, and troubleshooting.

UTILITIES

Mastering the Norton Utilities 5
Peter Dyson
400pp. Ref. 725-8
This complete guide to installing and using the Norton Utilities 5 is a must for beginning and experienced users alike. It offers a clear, detailed description of each utility, with options, uses and examples—so users can quickly identify the programs they need and put Norton right to work. Includes valuable coverage of the newest Norton enhancements.

Mastering PC Tools Deluxe 6
For Versions 5.5 and 6.0
425pp. Ref. 700-2
An up-to-date guide to the lifesaving utilities in PC Tools Deluxe version 6.0 from installation, to high-speed back-ups, data recovery, file encryption, desktop applications, and more. Includes detailed background on DOS and hardware such as floppies, hard disks, modems and fax cards.

Mastering SideKick Plus
Gene Weisskopf
394pp. Ref. 558-1
Employ all of Sidekick's powerful and expanded features with this hands-on guide to the popular utility. Features include comprehensive and detailed coverage of time management, note taking, outlining, auto dialing, DOS file management, math, and copy-and-paste functions.

Up & Running with Norton Utilities
Rainer Bartel
140pp. Ref. 659-6
Get up and running in the shortest possible time in just 20 lessons or "steps." Learn to restore disks and files, use UnErase, edit your floppy disks, retrieve lost data and more. Or use the book to evaluate the software before you purchase. Through Version 4.2.

Changing

Changing	Action Menu/Command	Function Key	Related Menu/Command	Pa
undo	Change/Undo	F1		5
redo (undo-undo)	Change/Redo	F2		5
erasing	Change/Erase	F3		5
copying	Change/Copy	F6		5
moving	Change/Move	F5		5
mirroring	Change/Mirror	Ctrl + F3		6
rotating	Change/Rotate	Ctrl + F5		6
scaling	Change/Scale	Ctrl + F6		6
stretching	Change/Stretch	F7		5
breaking	Change/Break	F4		5
chamfering	Change/Chamfer		Settings/Chamfer	6
filleting	Change/Fillet		Settings/Fillet	6
grouping	Change/Group	Alt + F9		6
ungrouping	Change/Ungroup	Alt + F10		6
editing text	Change/Text Editor			3.
changing properties	Change/Property		Settings/Property	7

Display

Display	Action Menu/Command	Function Key	Related Menu/Command	Pa
displaying the entire drawing	View/Zoom Full			1
zooming into an area	View/Zoom Box	F10		1
zooming to limits	View/Zoom Limits		Settings/Limits	1
zooming by factor	View/Zoom X			1
panning	• Use the scroll bars, or... • View/Pan	F8		2
redrawing the display	• Click the redraw button, or... • View/Redraw			
returning to previous view	View/Last View			1
viewing plot box area	View/Plot Box			